UEA MA Creativ
Anthologies 201
Non-Fiction

GW00853265

University of East Anglia

UEA NON-FICTION 2015

First published by Egg Box Publishing 2015

International © 2015 retained by individual authors.

This book is sold subject to the condition that it shall
not, by way of trade or otherwise, be lent, resold,
hired out, stored in a retrieval system, or otherwise
circulated without the publisher's prior consent
in any form of binding or cover other than that in
which it is published and without a similar condition
including this condition being imposed on the
subsequent purchaser.

A CIP record for this book is available
from the British Library.

UEA NON-FICTION 2015 is typeset in
Adobe Garamond. Titles are set in Mercury.

Cover photography from the photographic unit, UEA.

Printed and bound in the UK by Imprint Digital.

Designed and typeset by Sean Purdy.

Proofread by Sarah Gooderson.

Distributed by Central Books.

ISBN: 978-0-9932962-3-9

Acknowledgements

Thanks are due to the School of Literature, Drama and Creative Writing at UEA in partnership with Egg Box Publishing for making the UEA MA Creative Writing anthologies possible.

We'd also like to thank the following people:

Tiffany Atkinson, John Boyne, Andrew Cowan, Helen Cross, Giles Foden, Sarah Gooderson, Rachel Hore, Kathryn Hughes, Catrina Laskey, Bill Manhire, Jean McNeil, Natalie Mitchell, Jeremy Noel-Tod, Beatrice Poubeau, Rob Ritchie, Sophie Robinson, Helen Smith, Henry Sutton, Val Taylor, Ian Thomson, Steve Waters, Frances Wilson and Peter Womack.

Nathan Hamilton at Egg Box Publishing, and Sean Purdy.

Editorial team:

Rob Atkinson
Sohini Basak
Gill Blanchard
Jemma Carter
Joanna Graham
Alexis Kuzma
Elizabeth Lewis-Williams
Emma Victoria Miller
Molly Morris
Kayla Schmidt
Jade Tremblay
Chloe L Yeoh

CONTENTS

IAN THOMSON

Foreword

MY UEA CLASS, GIFTED, GOOD HUMOURED AND GENERALLY TOLERANT of me as a teacher, wanted to know what creative non-fiction is. The question set me thinking. Most people tend to know what is meant by biography; but creative non-fiction is a more sweeping term, that can accommodate any number of sub-genres from the personal essay to travel writing, reportage, memoir, anecdote, film script, notebook jottings, poetry and – why not? – wiki page entries. One thing it does have to be is well written: otherwise it would be *non-creative* non-fiction (polite for 'no good').

Creative non-fiction tends to blur the distinctions between fiction and non-fiction. Of course any work of writing is necessarily a fashioning and shaping of events. (The etymology of *fiction* from the Latin *fingere,* to 'mould' or 'contrive', is indicative.) But we do not expect non-fiction to distort in the same way; the truth is, it *does* distort: even biography distorts. Edmund Gosse's ground-breaking Edwardian memoir *Father and Son,* written when Gosse was nearly 60, reproduces conversations that purportedly took place when the author was a child. Had the conversations been made up? Most likely they had.

When is a life worth telling? BS Johnson, the London-born novelist and tireless chronicler of himself, put the most humdrum of autobiographical details into his 'truth-telling' novels of the 1960s. His non-fiction works of fiction might have been exercises in mere solipsistic spouting, were the writing not so good. (Even then, Johnson's cunningly fictionalised memoir *Trawl* fetched up in the Angling section of Foyles bookshop – an early example of an unsaleable literary hybrid.)

Most creative non-fiction writers make life more interesting than it is, blending truth with untruth (let us not call it 'lying'). Jonathan Meades, the British architectural correspondent and cultural commentator, conjured a vanished Salisbury of 1950s Cracker Barrel cheese adverts and Aertex shirts in his recent childhood memoir, *An Encyclopaedia of Myself.* How much of the memoir was embellished? The writing showed a novelist's hand at work in the use of Nabokov-like polysyllabic words ('gingivitic', 'leucous') and the heightened caricature.

Literary memoir in the Meades mould has been around for some time. Blake Morrison's *And When Did You Last See Your Father?*, published in 1993, recast Edmund Gosse's 1907 memoir as a very modern biography of self-disclosure and confession. These days, so-called 'life writing' tends to incorporate elements of anthropology, art criticism, travel, nature writing (sometimes known, somewhat comically, as 'wild writing') and other disciplines. Edmund de Waal's *The Hare with Amber Eyes* went beyond the stockades of conventional memoir to assimilate elements of allegorical pilgrimage, Jewish history, and the continental tradition of the moral essay.

De Waal was not the first to turn the raw material of his experience into a work of creative non-fiction. In 1984, Primo Levi's literary-scientific autobiography, *The Periodic Table*, reached the UK bestseller list alongside the thriller writer Dick Francis. Incredibly, the book had been turned down by no fewer than twenty-seven publishers in Britain before it was finally taken on. Such hybrid merchandise would never sell, editors feared. Things have changed considerably since then. Helen Macdonald's 2015 bestseller *H is for Hawk* was in many ways an exemplary hybrid. It was not autobiography exactly and it was not an ornithological treatise either. What *was* it? Peculiar in construction, audacious in conception, it was a marvel of biographical creative non-fiction.

Only now, three decades on, can we see that Primo Levi had been ahead of his time. Gabriel Weston's hospital memoir *Direct Red: A Surgeon's Story*, published in 2009, continued a tradition of scientific writing on mortality from the chemist-writer Primo Levi to the Norwich-based physician Sir Thomas Browne. Weston may not be a writer by vocation (not yet, anyway) but, like Helen Macdonald and others after her, she had much to say about human suffering and what Robert Louis Stevenson called 'the final insensibility of death'.

For reasons best known to them, my Biography and Creative Non-Fiction class presented me with a gift in the form of a T-shirt emblazoned with the words CAVALIER ATTITUDE [1]. My fondness for the Cavalier poets Robert Herrick and John Wilmot (Earl of Rochester) is perhaps known. But the T-shirt was intended to serve as a comment on my haphazard – if, I hope, invigorating – teaching methods. To my wife's bewilderment, I wear the T-shirt in bed (as a pyjama top). Some things you can't make up; the T-shirt is one of them.

London, June 2015

---

[1]: See 'I will call the police!' by Ian Thomson, *Spectator,* 4 April 2015

KATHRYN HUGHES

Introduction

THIS YEAR'S UEA'S NON-FICTION WRITERS SUCCEED IN MAKING THE world seem new again with their offering of rich and unexpected stories. Drawing on insider knowledge, Rob Atkinson explains how cruelly elephants can be treated in our zoos and circuses. Alison Baxter, meanwhile, unlocks the sad story of the great aunt whom she has disinterred from a past that includes both camels and canals. Harriet Clare explains how she fell silent in early adolescence, unable to utter a word about the things that mattered to her most. Historian Gill Blanchard recounts the story of 17th-century parliamentarian Vice-Admiral John Lawson, a rollicking tale of sea battles, imprisonment and barrels of pluck. Sara Fowler catches Nancy Mitford at the moment she moves from the novels that have served her so well into the unknown world of biography. Hannah Garrard takes us deep into the troubled heart of Liberia while Martha Henriques reveals the story of Emily Shore, a precocious girl naturalist of the 1830s. Laura Lovett tells us about working as a teacher with a group of young Americans who are more likely to end up in jail than graduate from high school. Ann Kennedy Smith shares her research on Caroline Reynolds Slemmer, a brave, beautiful heroine of the American Civil War who went on to marry a Cambridge classical scholar. Deborah Spring, meanwhile, explains how Elizabeth Freke, a miserable memoirist from the early 1700s, may in fact be deserving of our admiration as well as our pity. Finally, Kayla Schmidt tells us about the enchantment of being on the shores of Lake Metigoshe during dragonfly season. You'll wish you were there.

UEA MA Creative Writing Anthologies 2015: Non-Fiction

ROB ATKINSON

Sorting Out

Elephants in zoos and circuses are visitors' favourites,
but they are not always kindly treated.

'YOU KNOW THEY'RE KIND OF SQUARE-ISH TRIANGLES, DON'T YOU? THE jaw bones make the bottom angles and that big lump on the crown makes the top. And the sides and the front are flat.'

'Yes,' I said, wondering why Steve was describing an elephant's head. 'A massive great cube-triangle.'

An American zoo veterinarian of international reputation, Steve was sixty, tall and confident with a goatee beard and a Californian suntan. He was used to public speaking and television interviews, but now he was evasive, grappling with something uncomfortable. We were sitting at the end of a table in a pizza restaurant in downtown Kansas City, part of a group of animal activists, surrounded by laughter and light and good people. But Steve was shutting out all of that, and leaning towards me. He spoke quietly.

'Well this one's head wasn't square, and it wasn't grey like it should be, either. She didn't look right. I knew it as soon as I saw her, the morning after it happened.'

'What was wrong, Steve?'

'Her head was purple. And it was round, like a plum-coloured pumpkin. There were wounds on it and she kept putting her trunk up to touch them. She didn't move right, kind of slow. Normally she would've moved quickly – she was only nineteen, a teenager.'

I knew what was coming next. After thirteen years of work with captive elephants I'd met enough disturbed elephant handlers to know the story.

'They hit her for at least two days, maybe more, in the mornings before the public came in. Chained all four legs and pulled her over with a winch, then set to with axe handles – afterwards one said they'd been using home-run swings, like in baseball. The keepers had to take rests 'cause their arms and hands hurt so much.'

'Do you know why they did it?' – though I knew why. Many zoo elephants are traumatised and dangerous to humans. Because elephants breed so poorly in captivity, and because they live only half as long as they would in the wild, zoos buy baby elephants from dealers in Africa and Asia, where they are separated from their mothers and then through deprivation, chaining and beating made tractable and saleable. They are then exported to the world's zoos where, confined to enclosures one ten-thousandth the size of their ranges in the wild, eighty per cent of them become lame, as lame as factory-farmed chickens.

'She was difficult to handle, dangerous, like so many of them are, so they beat her to break her spirit and make her easier to manage.'

'What happened to her?' I asked.

'There was a hell of a fuss at the zoo. The city council got involved and activist groups too, but there wasn't enough evidence to prosecute for cruelty. She was moved out to a bigger park, and then eventually she went to Ashtree Zoo.'

Ashtree is one of a handful of zoos known for its progressive attitude towards elephants. Elephants are self-aware in a way that had long been thought to separate humans from animals, and they have the capacity for great joy and great sorrow. When an elephant dies its family will stand quietly over the body as if in mourning, and they may cover the body with vegetation. They will pick up the bones of their kin whilst ignoring those of other species. At Ashtree, the keepers understood their duty to such emotionally complex beings, and did their best to fulfil it.

'I've seen her there,' I said. 'She's looking good. A proper husbandry programme, no more sharp metal hooks to force obedience, no more axe handles. Just great keepers who try and give her an elephant's life instead of a prisoner's.'

Steve looked down at his half-finished pizza. 'She's OK now, kind of. As well as any elephant can be after that. I just wished I'd been able to stop it happening.'

Steve, a junior veterinarian at the time, had been sidelined when the zoo's management authorised the beating, a pattern often followed when there's someone on the team who wouldn't approve. The head keeper makes a convincing case to the zoo's director that the rogue elephant will wreck the herd's dynamics, and that it's in the elephant's own interests – if she doesn't behave she'll end up in solitary confinement, and no one will be able to go in with her any more, to look after her feet or give her medication. The head keeper knows how to seal his bid:

'If we don't sort her out, someone's going to get killed.'

The director, with a hundred other things to worry about, sees the zoo's good name tarnish. He doesn't want any of his staff killed, especially when he's been told so clearly that there's a way to avoid it. And, after all, he doesn't really know what *sort her out* means, hasn't heard this euphemism that is so common amongst elephant keepers. He's told what will happen: that the elephant will be pulled onto her side to teach her she's not as strong as she thinks she is; he sees the logic. He's told that if she lashes out with her trunk then that dangerous behaviour will have to be curtailed. This elephant's a bully, and the zoo's director knows the only thing that bullies respond to. He acquiesces.

I'd heard many stories like Steve's, of a beating with baseball bats that went on for eight hours, of an elephant rammed and crippled by a tractor. The worst was of a female tortured as only a female can be, with a steel brush connected to an electricity supply. How many of these tales are true I cannot say, but I have witnessed too much to make me wary of dismissing all or even most of them. I've seen the aftermath to a training session, when an elephant urinated in fear and blood ran down her trunk and flanks. Even regular training of elephants, rather than the last resort *sorting out* exercises, leaves its visible trace – the holes in the trunk where the metal hook was used too vigorously, and the way an elephant reacts when a keeper puts his hand in a pocket. The elephant remembers the last time that happened and an electric cattle prod was produced.

Some of these trainers are hard men, not caring about the real identity of the animals they are charged with looking after, or of what elephants really need to lead fulfilled lives. But most join starry-eyed, and then are swept along in a system of elephant management 4,000 years old that bestows considerable prestige on those who become expert, those able to handle even dangerous elephants safely. But very few keepers reach this level. Traditional elephant handling is a tough and dangerous job. There is great pressure placed on new recruits to do what is expected – they must not back down nor let the elephant establish dominance.

I have met elephant keepers at the beginnings of their careers, so shy they could hardly meet my eye, who within months were bristling with misplaced bravado, and using the same language as the old timers – all set to *sort out* the miscreants and *teach them good manners.* They are driven to meet the expectations of the lead keeper, who dominates them as they are expected to dominate the elephant. Meanwhile, the elephant watches the hierarchy amongst the keepers unfold; there is a widely held view amongst elephant handlers that it's usually the junior keepers who are attacked.

Only the hardened keep going with the brutal methods, and many keepers leave when their consciences get the better of them. Some become trapped in a loop of self-loathing and self-justification, wanting to move on whilst needing to stay and redeem themselves. John was one such. I met him at a conference at a zoo at the end of the nineties, just when the battle lines were finally being drawn between traditionalists and those demanding change. At John's request we arranged to meet in a café away from the conference hall where the other delegates were taking their break. At that time it mattered who you were seen talking to.

I arrived first and John joined me in the queue. He was pale, rather short and slight, with fair hair gelled back. His hands were thrust into the pockets of his jacket. He seemed wary – my disapproval of hardcore training methods was by this time well-known in the elephant keeping community – and when I asked what he wanted to drink he hesitated, as if he were being offered a bribe.

'I'll get these, John. Why don't you find somewhere to sit?'

I joined him at the table he'd chosen, which was as far away from other tables as he could get, and partially shielded by the imitation jungle vines that decorated the café's walls. He waited until I'd sat down and put his coffee in front him, then started talking.

'I *hate* the bastards!' John was sitting bent over in his chair, his hands in front of him as if simultaneously asking for forgiveness and ready to defend himself. He looked angry and desolate.

'Why?'

'Because I've seen what they do… but I'm not telling *you*!'

'There's no need to, John. But why do you want to work with elephants? Apart from anything else, it's fifty times more dangerous than the average job!'

'I want to do the right thing,' he answered.

'There's always room for improvement. We all make mistakes.'
Conversation with this haunted young man was difficult, forcing
platitudes.

'I didn't make any mistakes! We had to do it! You can't let elephants
get the better of you, you've got to sort them out!'

There it was again.

'*Sort them out?*' I asked.

'I *said* I'm not telling *you*! I could tell you... I'm not going to! I've seen
things that would make your hair stand on end but...'

'You're not telling me, right?'

At the time, I simply couldn't understand how fear-based training
of elephants could be contemplated. Those who supported it were
a minority, their approach at odds with standards of basic decency let
alone modern animal training practice. But I think I am wiser now.
Although very few elephant trainers are genuinely cruel, many, like
John, have done cruel things, seemingly abandoning the morals that
control their behaviour in other parts of their lives. I realise now that at
least sometimes they were driven by a belief that what they were doing
was right, and that in most cases it was a belief forced into them. The
eminent theoretical physicist Steven Weinberg, when contemplating
why good people do evil things, concluded *religion*, but maybe Richard
Dawkins has the more complete response, albeit to a different thesis.
Supplementing his own famous quote that anyone who didn't believe in
evolution was ignorant, stupid, insane or wicked, Dawkins added a fifth
category: '*characterised by a word like tormented, bullied, or brainwashed.
Sincere people who are not ignorant, not stupid, and not wicked can be
cruelly torn, almost in two.*'

*

When I left the zoo world in the late nineties it was to reassurances that
all was changing, yet afterwards I heard of incidents that intimated
that the tormenters were still active. The 5.00 am phone call to my hotel
room in Costa Rica from a former colleague in the UK about a young
male elephant that had just been viciously '*sorted out*', the whisper from
another that a newborn baby was already being lined up for separation
from its mother for training... I thought that at least the supply of
elephants from the wild was declining, owing to public disapproval, so

maybe elephants in captivity would dwindle too, and with them the pointless horror of their existences. But on 8 January 2015 the *Independent* announced that the Zimbabwean government was about to sell and ship baby elephants. Over the last two decades, more than a thousand elephants have been exported to the world's zoos.

Rob Atkinson worked in zoos and the RSPCA, and was Chief Executive Officer of an elephant sanctuary in the USA. He now writes and is working on establishing a vast, natural-habitat sanctuary on the Mediterranean coast for elephants rescued from the arenas and enclosures of Europe's circuses and zoos.

ALISON BAXTER

Forgotten Lives

A story of camels, puddings, love and loss.

IT WAS NOT UNTIL MY GRANDMOTHER DIED THAT I DISCOVERED SHE
had a sister. Now Amy's sapphires flash from my fingers as I type,
a constant presence at the edge of my consciousness. I treat them
carelessly – after making pastry I find fragments of dough lodged under
the stones, dulling their blue glow. As I scrub the ring, it conjures up a
glimpse of its owner.

I see her in the kitchen of her parents' hotel, in a high-necked blouse
and long skirt covered with a white apron, hands dusted with flour.
'Amy Smythe,' it says inside the front cover of her notebook, in looped,
fine-nibbed black handwriting, 'Balcarres, Echt'. And on the first page,
'Household Cookery, 12th October 1895.' The contents echo those of my
Penguin cookery book: solid British dishes like steak and kidney pie,
tomato soup, shortbread. Amy's scones are almost identical to mine,
although more than a hundred years separate us. Perhaps she too had to
clean scraps of dough from the sapphires.

Amy was sixteen when she started this book. Born in Aberdeenshire
in 1879, she was named after Amy Cunliffe-Brookes, the English wife
of the eleventh Marquis of Huntly. The Marchioness, herself childless,
wrote a gracious note to her former maid Martha Smythe:

'Mrs Smythe I am very glad you and the little baby are going on well…
I hope you will not receive this letter too late for I am quite willing you
should call the baby after my Christian name, & hope she will continue
to thrive.'

Martha probably hoped that her daughter would benefit from the
patronage of a great lady; she might even absorb some of the graceful

serenity that made Millais's portrait of Amy Brookes such a success when it was shown at the Royal Academy. But Amy Smythe was a tomboy.

Another image appears, sepia tinted this time. The two sisters are sitting together on the sofa in the drawing room. Amy is showing small Jean the photographs in a morocco-bound album with brass clasps.

'Look, Jeannie,' says Amy, 'this is my favourite. It's the great Sargano. When I grow up I'm going to be a lion tamer like him.' Sargano Alicamousa is a powerfully built black man in tight trousers, high boots and a leopard skin tunic; he has a resolute expression, like his eleven-year-old admirer.

It was 1890 and Lord George Sanger's Circus had arrived in the small town of Huntly, perhaps on its way to entertain the queen at Balmoral. The grey streets were filled with colour and noise as Mrs Sanger led the parade dressed as Britannia, reclining on an ornate gilded carriage next to a shabby, toothless lion. The circus camels were housed overnight in the stables of the Smythes' hotel. Amy crept out that evening and climbed into the long manger that held their fodder. She travelled from end to end, feeding and petting the unexpected guests, who gazed at her in haughty surprise and bared their yellow teeth. The circus people said it was a wonder she hadn't been bitten to death by the ill-tempered creatures, but Amy was fearless.

Lion taming was not, however, a realistic career for a young lady and Amy prepared for a suitably feminine future. In 1896 she graduated from the School of Domestic Economy in Aberdeen with a certificate stating her qualification to teach dressmaking 'in all its branches'. A contemporary photograph shows a girl with dark, wavy hair and the ridiculously small, corseted waist of the time. Her sleeves, puffed out like satin lanterns, have uncomfortably tight cuffs quite unsuited to an active life.

Family albums are full of ghosts that peep out of the shadows to tease us with hints of where we have come from and who we are. Reading Amy's notebook, I am looking without much hope for some insight into her feelings; although Jean became a published poet Amy was not a writer. But after *Lemon Curd* and *Victoria Sandwich* comes a blank page, and then *Love's Melody*: a heading which surely cannot refer to a pudding. I read on.

> 'A year ago, but one short year,
> We stood beneath the old oak tree,
> And I spoke words of love to thee
> Which thou wert glad at heart to hear.'

If Amy hoped marriage would compensate for a lost life of adventure, it was not to be. The lines continue:

'Life is all of love bereft ...
And now our love is with the dead'

I look down at the blue stones on my right hand. Tell me, Amy, did you copy this verse from a book or did you write it yourself? Who were you thinking of? I rub the smooth gold band of the ring but no answer appears. Amy's lost love is identified only by the initials WMW inscribed below the poem, and a date: 27/5/99. There is no one left now to remember the young man who gave her the sapphires: Walter? Wilfred? I imagine a tall, straight-backed soldier on his way to fight the Boers. He never came back; Amy never had a home and kitchen of her own. But she carried on cooking, and must have found some comfort in the activity, for the notebook ends not with regret but with *Crystal Palace Pudding* and *Tea Cakes*.

Amy faced the future with her usual courage, watching her younger sister grow up, take her place in local society, and meet potential suitors. A dusty collection of postcards and photographs is all that remains of the light-hearted correspondence between Jean and Andrew Ritchie Williamson, a student at Aberdeen University. Sometimes, I realise, the ghosts we glimpse are strangers with their own stories to tell; like coins lost down the side of a sofa, they appear when we are looking for something else.

Andrew's first card is dated 1904, the year Jean left school with her Higher Certificate but no clear plans for the future. His photograph shows an ascetic looking young man with wire-rimmed glasses, wearing an academic gown and holding a plumed mortar board. Perhaps he was a member of the informal club that met in the Smythes' hotel on summer Saturdays, when the parlour would fill with the smoke of a dozen pipes. Arts and medical students, lawyers, bankers, accountants, commercial travellers and trawl-owners cycled out from Aberdeen to the village of Echt to enjoy a glass of ale or a dram of whisky and settle the affairs of the nation in a gathering presided over by Jean's father.

Like Shakespeare's Beatrice and Benedict, the young couple trade insults that conceal a growing attraction. The morning after a party, an ironic note arrives.

'I do hope you enjoyed your little self at the ball. Was there anybody nice there? Anybody to suit your fastidious taste? Anybody to keep your sarcastic tongue between your teeth for three minutes on end?'

I imagine Andrew approaching Jean to request a dance. His stiff collar matches his rigid demeanour; he is not a confident dancer and anticipation is making him nervous. She is fanning herself after a strenuous eightsome reel.

'Oh dear, Mr Williamson,' she says. 'I'm afraid you are too late. My card is full. You need to be quicker on your feet if you're going to catch me.' And she laughs.

Andrew must have forgiven her, however, and continues to write. On a picture of the well-known Gaiety Girl Marie Studholme, who poses with an enticing curl over one eye, he scribbles a request:

'NB the curl. Please imitate.'

This earnest young man has literary aspirations and in a letter enclosing two 'exercises in versification' he conceals his anxiety about Jean's verdict on his efforts, claiming to have chosen the paper because it is 'easily burnt'. But his stronger feelings emerge.

'I can't rave in letters – print's too frigid & lacks the glance, the expression, the encouragement or the opposite that means everything – but at any rate let me remain, yours ever.'

Did Jean show the letter to Amy and ask her advice? There seems to have been a cooling in the friendship and after a long gap, a note arrives in February 1908 on notepaper headed Christ Church Oxford. It concludes ambiguously, 'Yours as ever (whatever that may mean) Andrew R Williamson.' He had passed for entry to the Indian branch of the Civil Service and while Amy would have relished the opportunity to ride elephants and hunt tigers, Jean must have had doubts about setting off for Bengal. In the end she did not have to decide.

The ambitious son of a Scottish schoolmaster, Andrew probably struggled to fit into the alien culture of Christ Church, that supremely aristocratic college with links to Eton, known to insiders as 'The House'. He was a classicist who had graduated from Aberdeen with first class honours and four prizes in Latin and Greek, so it was galling to find himself treated as a provincial nobody. How could he show that he belonged at Oxford? On 2nd May 1908, the river Cherwell was still swollen after the freak snowstorms of the previous month. The floods that had covered the meadows where cattle usually grazed were receding but there was still a lot of water. Andrew, ignoring the weather conditions and the fact that he was unable to swim, invited three fellow students to go punting.

They hired a boat from Salters' boat yard and worked their way up the Cherwell as far as Magdalen Bridge. Andrew was punting and the other three using the paddles. Suddenly they were caught by the current and one end of the boat hit a stone buttress with a huge jolt, swinging it round broadside to the river. It capsized, throwing all four occupants into the water. Two of the young men swam clear, while Andrew and his friend William Mackie, another non-swimmer, clung desperately to the hull of the punt. As it filled with water they lost their grip, grabbed hold once more, but were again swept off. Mackie was saved by one of the swimmers, who pushed him towards a willow tree that he used to pull himself out onto the bank, but Andrew Williamson had disappeared from sight. People on the bank of the Botanical Gardens watched in helpless horror while other boats rushed to the rescue, but in vain.

May morning in Oxford is known for its tragedies, when high-spirited students fuelled with champagne jump from Magdalen Bridge, breaking limbs and sometimes their necks. Andrew was equally reckless. At the inquest, a waterman employed by the University Humane Society testified that he searched for Mr Williamson until all hope was gone. He and his colleagues went on dragging the river for another eight days before the body was finally retrieved from Iffley Lock, a couple of miles downstream. A verdict of accidental death was returned with the Coroner commenting that:

'The men were at a time of life when, perhaps, their conduct was more characterised by courage than caution.'

Andrew was 24 years old.

Jean, like Amy, mourned the loss of her first love, but settled into a quiet domestic routine, comforted by the presence of her older sister. In 1911 she met a young English engineer and after some months they announced their engagement. The sisters had started to plan the wedding when suddenly one evening Amy complained of a headache and collapsed. She started vomiting and was put to bed. Her anxious sister sat beside her, holding her hand, reassuring her that she would soon be better. The doctor was summoned but Amy grew rapidly worse, losing the use of her limbs and drifting into unconsciousness. Shortly before midnight she died. On her death certificate the cause was given as 'spinal haemorrhage': a bleed into the brain. It was Christmas Eve.

At the age of 32 Amy was gone and Jean was left to face the future without her sister. In 1913 she married her engineer and moved south to London. My grandmother never spoke of her loss, but she kept the sapphire ring close for the next sixty years.

Alison Baxter has been a publisher, teacher and Chief Executive of a charity. This is part of a family history project where she uses everyday objects to tell the forgotten stories of ordinary Victorians. Alison is also writing a memoir about the independence of Vanuatu. She blogs at www.cautiousexplorer.wordpress.com.

GILL BLANCHARD

The Reluctant Kingmaker

An edited extract from the first chapter of a biography
of Vice-Admiral Sir John Lawson (1615-1665).

O N 13TH DECEMBER 1659, WITH THE ARMY CONTROLLING PARLIAMENT
and rioting on the streets of London, Vice-Admiral John Lawson led
22 warships into the Thames threatening to blockade the city in defence
of Parliament. 'As becomes Englishmen,' he declared, 'I am resolved with
my life and fortune to pursue the restoration of our liberties.'[1] Lawson
was about to play a pivotal role in the death throes of the republic for
which he had fought so hard since 1642.

Lawson had offered his services to the parliamentarian cause when
civil war broke out in 1642. 'Ever since,' he said, 'the Lord has kept my
heart upright to the honest interest of the nation, although I have been
necessitated twice to escape for my freedom and danger of my life.'[2]

Portraits show him with a receding hairline and long, curling hair.
Large round eyes look out with a steady gaze over a narrow and slightly
crooked nose, and firm, but not over full lips. Brief flashes of his
personality emerge from letters and diaries of contemporaries. 'A man of
probity,' thought parliamentarian Edmund Ludlow,[3] whilst Royalist Sir
Philip Warwick described him as 'most generous hearted and intelligent.'[4]
Renowned diarist Samuel Pepys generally thought well of Lawson despite
the occasional acerbic remark such as his being 'as officious poor man,
as any spaniel can be.'[5] Others considered him just a rough-mannered,
blunt-speaking tarpaulin – a common sailor – who had risen above his
station. These were mostly those who did not share his politics.[6]

Born in 1615, his home was at the lower end of Merchants' Row in
Scarborough, which ran alongside the castle dykes. Despite his reputed
'low parentage'[7] Lawson was a literate and articulate ship owner and

sea captain. His conversations with Edmund Ludlow during the crisis of 1660 reveal a trusting and optimistic nature in contrast to the steely resolve he displayed to the army leaders. He was the epitome of Cromwell's 'plain russet-coated captain who knows what he fights for, and loves what he knows.'[8]

Winter 1659: high winds, heavy rain and flooding swept across England and Scotland. Harvests were ruined for the third year in a row. The country's mood was desperate amidst fears of a return to the bloody conflicts of the 1640s and early 1650s. From on board his ship *The James*, Lawson wrote publicly to the Lord Mayor, aldermen and councillors of London, that he and his captains 'could not in all conscience tolerate the breach between Parliament and army that had come to the fore since October.' The cause which had cost them all 'so much blood and treasure' was facing 'utter ruin.'[9]

Radical elements in the army had taken control of government. Driven by religious and political scruples Lawson was desperately trying to restore a commonwealth government in whose defence he had already been imprisoned and exiled. This was, he asserted, a contest fought in Christ's own interest as well as that of his people. If Parliament could not be saved by friendly means he and his men would use the 'utmost endeavour for the removal of that force.'[10]

Appealing fervently to the Lord Mayor and City Council to withstand the designs of King Charles I's son – Charles Stuart – this deeply committed Puritan led his men into the Thames that grey December day on a point of principle. Parliament should never be subordinate. Not to the army. Not to any King. Nor to any Lord Protector.[11]

Lawson believed this could only be achieved by preserving the Rump Parliament which had come into existence eleven years before.[12] The Rump derived its name from the small number of Members of Parliament left in 1648 after Pride's Purge (after the MP who led it) forcefully removed those hostile to trying King Charles I for treason. Cromwell ushered in the commonwealth republic the following year. This is what Lawson was willing to fight and die for.

Lawson's fierce devotion to parliamentarianism had seen him navigate his way up the ranks until he was rewarded with the Vice-Admiralty by Cromwell in 1653. Later that same year Cromwell decimated the Rump by instigating another coup. Denouncing those he believed to have failed in reforming Parliament as whoremasters and drunkards, Cromwell copied the events of 1648 and had nearly half the Rump MPs removed by force and physically prevented from re-entering. Within months Parliament and the Commonwealth were reduced to bare bones and Oliver Cromwell had established himself as Lord Protector.

Lawson publicly supported the Levellers who agitated for a radical egalitarian society (at least for men). He was rumoured to be one of the religious subversives known as Anabaptists as well as associating with the Fifth Monarchist Movement – many of whom believed Christ would descend to earth in 1666. Lawson had become tainted in Cromwell's eyes despite the many honours previously bestowed on him.[13]

There is no doubt where Lawson's sympathies lay. For him the 'just foundations of a godly government'[14] could only be achieved through freedom of worship and the abolition of tithes – a tax which maintained Church of England clergymen.[15] In very modern sounding terms Lawson also proposed making comfortable provision for disabled seamen and the widows and orphans of serving sailors, creating jobs for the able bodied poor and giving financial aid to those 'too lame and impotent to work.'[16]

Here we catch a glimpse of what shaped Lawson. He spent a large portion of his life in a town whose fortunes – even its sights and smells – were dominated by the treacherous North Sea, learning his trade transporting coal from Sunderland. Perhaps it was personal experiences that led him to call for the abolition of the pressgangs that forced men into the army and navy. He was intimately concerned with the welfare and morals of his men. Almost unique amongst seventeenth-century naval officers in not having been a gentlemen soldier first, his manner certainly found favour with ordinary sailors.[17]

In April 1657, his links to schismatic republican groups resulted in Lawson's imprisonment in the Tower. Upon release he returned to Scarborough with his wife Isabella and daughters. During their two-year exile he rented the Garlands fields on the edge of town and turned to farming.[18]

Oliver Cromwell died in September 1658. Although thousands mourned just as many others celebrated, one can only wonder if Lawson honoured this man who also fought for parliamentarianism, despite their differences. Or, did Lawson believe Cromwell to be as much a traitor as those who had turned to the Royalists?[19]

Oliver Cromwell's son Richard succeeded him and the fault lines between moderate and extremist republicans opened. Revolutionary ideas were abroad again. The army was owed months of back pay and was accused of giving guns and swords to Anabaptists and Quakers.

By May 1659, Republican army leaders had forced Richard Cromwell out and reinstalled the Rump Parliament. The new regime declared it would re-establish a commonwealth without a single ruler. They brought Lawson back from exile and reinstated him as Vice-Admiral with command of six frigates. John's political regeneration had begun.[20]

This new Parliament was no more popular than the one it replaced. Royalist plotters seized their opportunity, encouraged by Charles Stuart arguing that the dissolving of Richard Cromwell's Parliament was a just and proper reason for 'all men to betake themselves to their arms.'[21] His informers reported that 'the common soldier's discourse... is that they are worse under this Parliament than they were before.'[22] By June plans were well underway for a Royalist rising against the Rump, but the plot was uncovered in July. Suspected sympathisers were interrogated and people's homes searched, provoking immense hostility to the government.[23]

On 12th October 1659, Lawson's world turned upside down.[24] He was at the naval base at Rye in Sussex when, after months of conflict, the Rump attempted to limit the army's power. The next day, in an echo of the events of 1648 and 1653, the army in London under John Lambert's command marched to Westminster, drove the MPs and the Speaker out, locked the doors and set guards to prevent them re-entering. They did so in the name of the republic.

A military dictatorship was now running the country. 'Anger began to boil to an exceeding great height.'[25] 'What governance we shall have next is not yet known,'[26] wrote the Royalist spy Mr Samborne. By the first week of December the country was at 'the mercy and impulse of a giddy, hot-headed, bloody multitude.'[27] Soldiers patrolled the streets of London.

Then, on 5th December, came a surge of violence as city apprentices petitioned for the removal of the army. Troops and the young protestors from every trade and city guild clashed near Whitehall. It is likely that Samuel Lawson, the son of John's cousin, and apprentice grocer to his father in Lyme Street[28] was one of those hurling stones, tiles and turnips. The soldiers shot them down, killing several and wounding over thirty. In the following days soldiers pulled down city gates and carried grenadoes – an explosive shell – into St Paul's Cathedral and elsewhere. Butchers pretending to play football attacked the guard inside Whitehall. The prisons filled.[29]

This was John Lawson's moment. Declaring himself for the Rump and against the army, he and his fleet arrived at Gravesend at the mouth of the Thames on 13th December. Londoners boarded up their shops and homes or fled to the shires for safety. 'We entreat you, as servants of the Commonwealth,' Lawson wrote to city officials the same day, 'take off the force that is now put upon Parliament… My men and I will not acquiesce to the army ruling government. The Rump must be allowed to sit again.'[30]

Three hundred and fifty thousand Londoners were dependent on the river for trade and transport. Terrified of Lawson's power to paralyse the city, Lawson's friend Sir Henry Vane was dispatched downriver to 'stroke' him.[31] A satirical account of their meeting has Vane bemoaning Lawson's ingratitude at leaving them 'in the suds.'[32] Rejecting Vane's overtures, Lawson's duty was, he said, to oppose all 'pernicious designs' to convert 'the supreme power of the nation into the hands of the army.'[33]

This then was the crux. All these men had fought on the same side. Together they had brought into being the Rump Parliament that Lawson swore to protect. Now his former companions had swept it away. Both sides believed they were protecting the Commonwealth. The only thing they agreed on was no monarchy. Lawson was forceful. If the Rump was not restored and the army brought back under control his forces would bring 'them to account for all their horrid perjuries, breach of trust, blasting, and abusing of the nation.'[34] He was declaring for the Commonwealth republic as created in 1649.

Christmas Eve 1659: London's Common Council had appealed to General Monck, Commander-in-Chief of the Army in Scotland, to support Parliament. This appeal and Lawson's letters and declaration in defence of the Rump had been printed onto broadsheets and widely circulated.[35] Now, the ordinary soldiers of the London regiments turned against their commanders and protested outside Whitehall. Army rule collapsed and on Boxing Day the Rump was restored. The Speaker and MPs walked together to Parliament to applause from the soldiers who had just days before kept them from sitting.[36]

Samuel Pepys began his journal on 1st January 1660, noting how 'Lawson lies still in the River'[37] and the army officers were forced to yield.[38] Snow fell hard and the city froze as Monck and his army made their way south.[39] After being publicly thanked in Whitehall for his fidelity and good service, Lawson was granted a pension of £500 a year.[40]

Within three months of his bold stand to defend the Commonwealth, Lawson had forsaken it and become a reluctant kingmaker.

1: Lawson, John. 22 Dec. 1659: *A Narrative of the Proceedings of the Fleet, giving an Account of what hath passed since their arrival at Gravesend; between divers hon. Members of parliament and vice admiral Lawson etc.* London; Lawson, John. 13 & 21 Dec. 1659: *Two Letters from Vice-Admiral John Lawson and the Commanders of the Fleet to the Lord Mayor, Aldermen and Common-Councilmen of the City of London.* Copies at British Library.

2: Letter. *John Lawson to Sir Henry Vane*, 1653. In. Binns. Jack. 2000: *Sir John Lawson* in *Oxford Dictionary of National Biography*. Vol. 32.

3: Firth, C.R., Ed. 1894: *The Memoirs of Edmund Ludlow, lieutenant-general of the horse in the army of the commonwealth of England 1625-1672.* Vol. II. Clarendon Press, p.176.

4: Warwick, Sir Philip. 1702. Reprint 1813: *Memoirs of the Reign of King Charles the First.* Edinburgh, p.476.

5: Latham, Robert and Matthews, William, Eds. 1970: *The Diary of Samuel Pepys. Vol. I. 1660.* Bell & Hyman.

6: *A Calendar of the Clarendon State Papers Preserved in the Bodleian Library.* Vol. IV. 1657-1660. 1932: Eds. Routledge, F.J. and Firth, Sir Charles. Clarendon Press; Binns. *Ibid*; Penn, Granville. 1833: *Memorials of the professional life and times of Sir William Penn from 1644 to 1670.* Vol. 2. London: J. Duncan. p.185.

7: Hinderwell, Thomas. 1832: The History and Antiquities of Scarborough. 3rd Edition. Bye, London.

8: Hunt, Tristram. 2002: *The English Civil War: At First Hand.* Weidenfeld and

Nicolson, p.xii.

9: Lawson. *A Narrative* & *Two Letters*. *Ibid*.

10: Lawson, John. 13 Dec 1659: *A declaration of Vice-Admiral John Lawson, commander in chief of the fleet in the narrow seas by authority of parliament, with the commanders of the several ships now with him in the Downes, in order to the removal of the interruption that is now put upon the Parliaments the 13th of October last*. London. Copy at British Library.

11: Lawson. *Letter*. 21 Dec. 1659. *Ibid*.

12: *Ibid*.

13: Binns. *Ibid*.

14: Lawson. *A Declaration*. *Ibid*.

15: Lawson. *Ibid*; Binns. *Ibid*. Burke's Peerage 107th Edition. 2003.

16: *Ibid*.

17: Letters from John Lawson [various collections]; Calendars of State Papers. 1650s & 1660s; Lawson. *A Declaration*. *Ibid*; Binns. *Ibid* Burke's Peerage. *Ibid*.

18: Hinderwell, *Ibid*, p.230.

19: Binns. *Ibid*.

20: *Ludlow. Ibid*, p.92.

21: Letter. 20 June 1659: *The King to Mr. Mordaunt*. In. Clarendon's State Papers. Vol. III.

22: Letter. 30 June 1659: *Mr Samborn to the Lord Chancellor Hyde*. Clarendon SP. *Ibid*.

23: Letters. 1 July 1659: *Mr. Rumbold to the Lord Chancellor Hyde* & 1 Sept 1659: *Mr. Mordaunt to the King*. Clarendon SP. *Ibid*.

24: The phrase 'world turned upside down' was first used in a protest ballad in the 1640s and in subsequent political speeches to describe the effects of the civil war.

25: *The Monthly Intelligencer*. Dec. 1659 - Jan. 1660.

26: Letter. 14 Oct. 1659: *Mr Samborne to the Lord Chancellor Hyde*. Clarendon SP. *Ibid*.

27: Parkinson, R. Ed. 1852: *Autobiography of Henry Newcome*. Chetham Soc. In. Hill. Christopher. 1972. Reprint 1991. *The World Turned Upside Down: Radical Ideas During The English Revolution*. Penguin, p.345.

28: London Apprenticeship Abstracts, 1442-1850. Transcript by Cliff Webb from records at Guildhall Library, London.

29: *Monthly Intelligencer*. *Ibid*.

30: Lawson. *Letter*. 13 Dec. 1659: *Ibid*; Penn. *Ibid*, p.185.

31: Penn, *Ibid*, pp.184-186; *A Calendar*. *Ibid*, p.488.

32: *Sir Harry Vane's last sigh for Committee of Safety, etc. with the Right Honourable Vice-Admiral John Lawson, 17 Dec. 1659*. Copy at British Library.

33: Penn. *Ibid*, p.185.

34: *Ibid*, pp.189-190.

35: Albemarle, George Monck, Duke of. 1660: *A Letter of advice to his excellencie the Lord General Monck*. London. Copy Bodleian Library; Anon. 1660: *Letters to the council of state, from the commissioners of the militia... and a letter from the Lord Montague...* Printed by Abel Roper and Thomas Collins, London. Copy Henry E. Huntingdon Library and Art Gallery.

36: *Ibid*, pp.194-195.

37: *Pepys. Ibid.* p.1.

38: *Ibid.* p.1.

39: *Ibid*, pp.3-17.

40: Penn. *Ibid*, pp.194-195.

Gill Blanchard is a historical biographer, professional genealogist and house historian. She has three guides published by Pen and Sword Books and a biography of an 1830s scandal due out. She is writing a biography of parliamentarian Vice-Admiral Sir John Lawson. A staunch republican, once imprisoned by Cromwell for radicalism, he switched sides in 1660 and helped change the course of history.

HARRIET CLARE

Words After Speech

I WAS TOLD NOT TO TALK.

'Now then,' the housemistress said, perched on the bed of someone else's child, 'I think it's best if you don't mention your parents too much – and try not to make a fuss when you're being picked up this evening.'

I nodded. She straightened her skirt to hide the pale hem of her petticoat. The boarders were having tea, and the dormitory was deserted. Six small beds stood ready for the evening.

I sat opposite, beside another girl's stuffed animals.

'This is the first time most of the boarders will have been away,' she said, 'and some have only just turned 11 – so they might get a bit homesick-y.' She picked up a stray scrunchie from the floor.

'We want you to feel welcome, of course – but we haven't had any day girls before,' she paused, 'so this will be a learning curve for all of us.'

*

For the first two weeks of term the boarders were not allowed to call home. Instead, they wrote letters to their parents in Chelsea – and arrived in chapel red-eyed every morning. After this hiatus, they were allowed ten minutes, each week, to use the public pay phone in the corridor.

I had never seen anything like it. When I left home, years later, it was a timely escape from family life with kid-siblings – not this terrible exile.

The housemistress had been right: I couldn't mention my parents. I was one of only three day girls in a year group of a hundred, and life at home became unspeakable.

Each morning, my father would drop me at school just after 7am, before catching the train into London. We ate breakfast in the numb dark before dawn, and drove along the motorway listening to Classic Gold on medium wave radio: *Nights in White Satin* and *Unchained Melody*. He smelt of aftershave, and kept an electric razor in the glove box. He would shave in the school car park, stretching his skin in the rear view mirror.

'Have a good day,' he would say with a smile, 'work hard and earn lots of money.'

I would join the boarders in the dining room. Buoyant with the morning's letters, or tearful – linking arms in solidarity – they talked of the moments I had missed overnight. Initially I tried to join in, laughing at everyone else's jokes, as the conveyor of the industrial toaster turned.

I soon gave up. Chapel marked the start of the school day – and it was easier to fall into line in the cloisters, than listen to talk of the night before.

For two years I hid in the boot room during breakfast. Rows of metal cages, and heavy cloaks – used only once a year for the carol service – made it an easy place to disappear. Trunks and tuck boxes were stacked to the ceiling and the air smelt of sweat and linseed oil. No one was ever there for more than a few minutes – to collect a lacrosse stick or textbook.

'Oh, hi Hattie,' they would say, 'I didn't see you there.'

'Yeah, sorry, I was just leaving,' I'd reply.

'Cool.'

No one knew I had been standing there for an hour, pretending I had just arrived. My days were bookended by awkward pauses in the boot room. And as the term went on the silence began to swell – until I found I had nothing to say.

*

Selective mutism normally occurs in much younger children. Initially it can seem quite normal: the toddler tearfully clinging to his mother's legs and shying away when asked his name. But while other children adapt to school life and begin to speak – reaching for the Play-Doh and smiling – the selective mute will retreat into silence, meeting the world with a blank expression; flat and unreadable, as if they aren't quite there.

At school I would answer direct questions from teachers, or other girls, but I lost the art of conversation. Weeks would pass when I said little more than, 'Yeah. Cool. Thanks.'

I was never bullied – just ignored.

My parents didn't know what was happening. Like most selectively mute children, I remained articulate and talkative at home. I was too ashamed to tell them I didn't have any friends.

In early studies, speechless children were labelled obstinate, difficult, and taciturn. Their silence was mistaken for strong will, rather than fear. But silence stalks trauma – and childhood mutism is now understood to be triggered by anxiety. It is a way of both controlling and escaping a chaotic world.

*

My siblings and I always knew that sending us to school had been a sacrifice: my father re-routing his life, and driving miles cross-country to drop me at the gates. We understood that the school fees were unimaginably high, and we had to work hard to justify the investment.

Then my father lost his job.

It felt as though I was peeping through my fingers at a horror film – unable to see the screen – but knowing something terrible was happening. The house became cold. The empty rooms suddenly dark. After school I would sit watching *999* with the sound down, listening to the adult voices next door. I saw Michael Buerk explain how to escape if your car should fall into a canal – but I could never make out the words coming from the kitchen. All I could hear was their anger.

The fights became louder, longer. One afternoon I encountered my father crying in the study, pressing his fingers against his eyes, his mouth hanging empty. He turned the swivel-chair away as I walked past. We heard doors slam, and my mother would drive off for hours without telling us where she was going.

'Don't worry,' my father would say, a hand on my shoulder, 'it's my fault. She'll be back.'

That year my grandmother arrived to take care of my baby brother, and my mother retrained as a teacher. She would sit in the living room wrapped in a blanket, reading textbooks, with the curtains closed.

I stopped sleeping. I would lie awake until the early hours worrying about the day ahead, listening to my baby brother screaming. One night I peered into my parents' room looking for comfort.

'What now?' my mother asked. She hadn't yet slept – run ragged by the redundancy and a toddler, and the prospect of her mother moving in. 'What can you possibly want now, Harriet?'

My father led me downstairs and we slid on wellies over our cold feet and pyjamas. We walked hand in hand along the lane, behind the house, where he had taught me to ride a bike – running along behind, and never telling me when he had let go of the saddle.

'I'm sorry,' he said, and squeezed my hand. I looked at my wellies. There was nothing to say.

Silence closed over the house. The shame had become almost palpable. Every morning my father wore a suit for the school run, but the car no longer smelt of aftershave. We were told not to tell anyone outside the family what was happening.

'Blood runs thicker than water,' my mother had said, 'and people don't need to know about Daddy.'

*

At school we were learning about the Christian work ethic. The scripture teacher made it sound so simple. 'Consider the lilies of the field,' she told us. 'They neither toil nor spin, yet even Solomon in all his glory was not arrayed as one of these.' It was the first time I had viewed an adult with contempt – her image of unemployment was nothing like the creeping despair in our unheated house. As she stood at the front of the class, my eyes were level with her crotch, pinched in tight trousers.

'You don't have a fucking clue,' I thought, relishing the weight of the adult expletive. But I never said anything – and so the gulf between home and school grew wider.

My favourite moments were when I didn't have to do anything, and there were no expectations of me. I yearned for the three minutes of silent prayer in chapel every morning when I could sit with my head down in the crook of my arm, the ridges of my jumper embossed on my forehead.

*

Some children grow out of mutism. The majority are cured by careful therapy. An early therapeutic method was to encourage the child to use other people's words to find their own. In one case a boy was presented with a tape recorder and a microphone. Rather than attempting conversation, he was asked to record a few lines of poetry. The therapist closed the door and waited in the corridor. At first the child whispered in the empty room, stuttering and stumbling over the lines. But he was heartened by hearing his voice on tape, and the next recording was slightly louder, until eventually he didn't need the microphone, but sat opposite the doctor and read the words out loud.

*

It is a hot July evening. Everyone has taken their ties off. The sixth form wear flip-flops with their school skirts. The leggings and polo neck I am wearing are camouflage against the black-box stage. I am hands, and feet, and face.

The annual speech and drama competition is held at the end of the summer term. During the day I have read again and again in knockout rounds, and now the whole school has gathered in the theatre for the final.

I am sweating under the roll neck, and can feel a soft fold of flesh against the waistband of my leggings. I fiddle with an elastic band, wrapping it around my fingers and stuffing it down my sleeve to still the anxiety.

I know I can speak someone else's words. I mutter them under my breath, the elastic sticky in my palm. My mother has always read to me, and as a young child I would fall asleep listening to her speaking in the voices of people that never existed: Moon Face and the Psammead. She took me out of school when I was eight to compete in declamation exams, and read to me in the slow hours of insomnia. The words of others are important.

I have chosen the poem from a collection provided by the drama teacher. It is about death – a trauma greater than anything I have experienced. A serious and grown-up loss that matters. I know the words by heart.

I am the youngest person in the final. Everyone else in my year is watching – high in the auditorium – lost behind the lights. There is a sign saying, 'Finalist' taped to the floor by my seat. I stand in the centre of the stage.

'Childhood,' I begin, 'is not from birth to a certain age and at a certain age
    The child is grown, and puts away childish things.' I pause.
    'Childhood is the kingdom where nobody dies.
    To be grown up, is to sit at the table with people who have died,

who neither listen nor speak;
Shout at them, get red in the face, rise,
Drag them up out of their chairs by their stiff shoulders and shake
them and yell at them;
They are not startled, they are not even embarrassed; they slide
back into their chairs.'[1]

The hall is silent. The plastic seat is still warm when I sit down to watch the older girls perform their pieces. I collect my trophy during prize-giving the following week, my neck reddening to the applause. After the competition I stay the night on a spare bed in one of the dormitories, and count the glow stars on the ceiling as I listen to other people breathing.

It took years to trust people as I did before the mornings in the boot room, and the blood that was thicker than water. But that night was the beginning of my recovery, because it proved I had a voice. Looking back, I am still grateful for the poem, as it articulated the need to speak while we can – before we are face to face with the silent dead.

1: Edna St Vincent Millay, excerpt from 'Childhood is the Kingdom Where Nobody Dies' from Collected Poems. Copyright 1934, © 1962 by Edna St Vincent Millay and Norma Millay Ellis. Reprinted with the permission of The Permissions Company, Inc., on behalf of Holly Peppe, Literary Executor, The Millay Society, www.millay.org.

Harriet Clare is an award-winning journalist and film-maker, who is currently writing a memoir exploring the myth and medical history of speechlessness. She is also working on a biography of the lesbian 1920s music hall icon Gwen Farrar. She has published short fiction and memoir and lives in London.

SARA FOWLER

From Alconleigh to Versailles: Nancy Mitford's Emergence as a Biographer

NANCY MITFORD FOUND HERSELF WITH A DILEMMA IN 1952. SHE HAD just published *The Blessing*, after a string of bestselling novels. She had settled in Paris, where she had followed the man she believed was the love of her life. Established in a beautiful apartment on Rue Monsieur, it seemed she had every reason to be happy.

For the first time since her twenties, Nancy had no plans for another novel. Her social engagements and a column for *The Times* would keep her busy, but that wasn't enough, financially or intellectually. When she began writing, the goal was to supplement her meager income, but she discovered the joy of the process as she wrote. With her first major success, *The Pursuit of Love*, Nancy had established real capital. Having grown up with the financial crises Selina Hastings calls 'an integral part of Nancy's childhood,' Nancy was deeply conscious of money.[1] No amount of capital could ever let her feel secure. Now independent, she still had a visceral horror of poverty.

From her first novel, Nancy was preoccupied by questions of love. As her romantic life grew more painful, she used her novels to ask correspondingly difficult questions about love's meaning. Writing about an Englishwoman accepting Gallic infidelity in *The Blessing*, she asked and answered the last question she needed to answer through fiction. This began the end of her career as a romantic novelist.

After considering a 'shameless & complete autobiography', she settled on a biography of Madame de Pompadour, Louis XV's mistress.[2] In this book, Nancy adopted a character from her new country as her subject. Her Francophilia remained undimmed, but her romanticism had lost its naive intensity. Nancy wrote *The Pursuit of Love*, *Love in a Cold Climate*, and *The Blessing* to explore personal dilemmas, explaining the resonance and insight that distinguish them from her cruder early novels, which lack the melancholy, yearning romanticism that tinges even their successors' giddiest jokes with sad significance.

Her relationship with Gaston Palewski, in which she was always supplicant and pursuer, had changed. He remained involved with other women, devoting less of his attention to Mitford each year. While he had tolerated her affections, the romantic and sexual aspect of their relationship had diminished. Lisa Hilton writes in *The Horror of Love* that during Mitford's first post-war years in Paris, while 'they remained discreet, they could now enjoy some sort of a life together, and within their circle they could be perceived as a couple.'[3] Mitford had joined Palewski without an invitation. Their romantic involvement was emotionally asymmetrical, but she persisted. Unlike her 'continuing love for a faithless man,' however, her writing demanded radical change.[4]

She turned to the last period of history she regarded as truly civilized: eighteenth-century France. 'The four main pastimes,' Mitford writes of Versailles, 'were love, gambling, hunting, and the official entertainments,' the occupations that have traditionally occupied the aristocracy.[5] This setting epitomized the values that were Nancy's birthright as an aristocrat and her choice as an aesthete.

One wonders what affinity Nancy could have for the middle-class mistress of a French king. The answer may lie in the nature of Madame de Pompadour's relationship with Louis XV. Nancy attributed Pompadour's influence over Louis XV and his court to the strength of a relationship that transcends physicality, which Nancy suggests may have reinforced Pompadour's influence.

> If Madame de Pompadour were not physically in love with the King, being constitutionally incapable of passion, it would not be too much to say that she worshipped him; he was her God. She had other interests and affections, but she made them all revolve round him; rarely can a beautiful woman have loved so single-mindedly.[6]

Madame de Pompadour provided Nancy with an example of a fulfilling relationship past the stage of passion, a profoundly comforting idea. Their relationship had shifted from an affair fueled by wartime tensions to a lopsided friendship, far less rewarding than the love she had expected. She had mistaken the excitement of a wartime fling for a grand passion and found herself living with the consequences in the less heady atmosphere of peace. Still, Nancy refused to stray from her course.

Even in 1946, at the beginning of her relationship with Palewski, Nancy must have seen signs of his indifference. Writing to Evelyn Waugh, 'seized with insomnia,' she outlined a humiliating incident:

> I went to a ball at Princess de Bourbon-Parme's, duly binged up as one is before balls, with champagne, black coffee & so on. Well we hadn't been there 2 minutes before the Colonel said we couldn't stay on acc/ of the great cohorts of collaborators by whom we were surrounded, & firmly dumped me home.[7]

The combination of caffeine, alcohol, and romantic anxiety is potent enough to fuel weeks of insomnia, but Nancy attributed it to having 'made enemies for life' among hostesses.[8]

Waugh responded, 'Collaborationists my foot. Does it not occur to you, poor innocent, that continental colonel went back to the aristocratic ball & that while you lay sleepless with your fountain pen, he was in the arms of some well born Gestapo moll?'[9]

Waugh's literary advice was patronizing and pedantic, but candid personal advice he offered Nancy sometimes proved helpful. From his explanation of Hamish St Clair Erskine's homosexuality in the 1920s to illuminations of Palewski's shortcomings, Waugh's advice offered Nancy realism and perspective, which she sometimes ignored.

The assertion made by some critics that her description of Madame de Pompadour as a physically cold woman is veiled autobiography may be unwarranted. However, the idea that Pompadour provided a model of what Nancy's relationship with Palewski might become is not. The image of a woman who became her former lover's confidante and advisor must have been attractive. She refused to let Palewski's emotional coolness diminish her devotion. *Madame de Pompadour* provided a channel for her intense energy and a lens through which to interpret her personal trials.

She wrote to a colleague to ask for a few sources. She was 'starting from scratch' but would 'try and do as little Bibliothèque nationale as possible because my poor brain doesn't function much in such places.'[10] Still, to Evelyn Waugh, she wrote that she is 'working hard', and compares her *Madame de Pompadour* to Waugh's *Edmund Campion: Jesuit and Martyr*, published in 1935.[11]

Waugh responded by correcting her grammar in a recent article, warning, 'You really must be careful now that you are doing a work of scholarship.'[12] Despite corrections better left to Mitford's editors, even Waugh admits the intensity and dedication evident in *Madame de Pompadour*.

Nancy's style remained consistent across genres and decades, staying bright in *Madame de Pompadour*. Mitford saw the beauty and the 'ridiculous side' of French court life, maintaining a balance between humor and poignancy.[13] Some critics of the time alleged that Mitford's biographies were about her family, calling the book a return to Alconleigh through a study of Versailles, set in Cotswolds stone but dressed in gilt-and-pastel rococo style. She found this amusing, mentioning it in various letters.

Mitford saw no reason to alter a style that had ensured her success throughout *Madame de Pompadour* and subsequent biographies. 'The fact is, with me, my love of shrieking is greater than my *amour propre*. My skin is thick. And, great protection, I never can take myself very seriously as a *femme de lettres*,' she writes to Waugh around this period.[14]

Nancy's writing reveals assurance, a strong work ethic despite self-proclaimed laziness, and a cultivated intellect. She professed weakness as a writer, but her tone owes more to versatility of subject and consistency of style. Her voice remains accessible, girlish, and unwilling to concede to scholarly or literary convention at the expense of freshness or objectivity. (Her attachment to France shines through, as does her respect for Madame de Pompadour's use of traditional femininity in politics.)

Waugh praises later biographies: 'You write so deceptively frivolously that one races on chuckling from page to page without noticing the solid structure.'[15] Writing 'deceptively frivolously' may not have been the key to scholarliness as defined by the Victorians they read in their youth, but ensures a pleasant time for the reader and an appeal to a broad market. She sounds like an excellent conversationalist, not a lecturer.

Mitford spent her life honing this voice, designed to help her breeze (or appear to breeze) through any amount of pain. A little sparkle can make cold houses, bereavement, and disappointed love bearable and presentable, with an emphasis on the latter. Nancy prioritized maintaining what she called 'the shop front'.[16] This drove much of her humor, and may have fueled her exploration of a relationship in which she saw distinct parallels to her own. In criticizing Nancy's work, it seems easy to draw parallels: this character is Palewski, that is Nancy herself, and there is Stephen Tennant peeking from the next page in an outré outfit. Her emotional engagement remains oblique, but searching for problems Nancy is trying to solve in her own life when reading her work is fairer than identifying anecdotes or matching up characters from her life to characters in her work. It certainly provides more stimulation for the reader.

Nancy did not mention the bond between biographer and subject in her correspondence. Examining her relationship to Pompadour isn't the same as demonstrating that Lord Berners provided the model for Lord Merlin in *The Pursuit of Love*. In resembling psychoanalytic criticism, it would have earned Nancy's scorn, but it may provide a lens through which to examine her attachment to Palewski. Her attempts to preserve this relationship offer some insight into her perspective on Madame de Pompadour. *Madame de Pompadour* was a means of writing autobiographically without writing autobiography and cannot be read as direct representation of her life. She wrote to several friends about a memoir, but her fear of self-revelation thwarted her at every stage. Nancy wrote to understand the world and her own otherwise inaccessible psychological landscape as well as to entertain, but the shop front remained intact.

After a prolonged debate, Nancy would soon turn down a lucrative contract to work as a screenwriter in Hollywood so she could stay in Paris:

> So I decided against Hollywood, after 2 days of slight hysteria. I realized that it's not a question of whether you need me or not – the point is I can't live without you. I should be too miserable & it can't be right to make oneself miserable for dollars.[17]

Nancy was not indispensable to Palewski, but she had found a man she could make the center of her world. She could not imitate the model of closeness stemming from feminine devotion that she had observed in *Madame de Pompadour*, but she seems to have found such devotion worthwhile in itself. She found the genre in which she would continue to shine: sparkling, impeccably researched biographies undimmed by traditional scholarly self-seriousness. Mitford continued writing biography after *Madame de Pompadour*, beginning with 1957's *Voltaire in Love*, an examination of Emilie du Chatelet's relationship with Voltaire. With considerable success, she revisited eighteenth-century France, focusing on the intersection of love and intellectual life.

Madame de Pompadour earned less critical recognition than its successors *Voltaire in Love*, *The Sun King*, and *Frederick the Great* would, but it marked the beginning of Nancy's new career as surely as *Don't Tell Alfred* heralded the end of her time as a novelist. Less surprising than Nancy's attempt to refashion herself as a biographer is how little of her style, her method, or her mind required reinvention.

Her literary output only decreased when a mysterious cancer incapacitated her. Until pain forced her to stop writing, Nancy Mitford maintained her ability to understand the whole from a few carefully observed parts. Her attunement to the absurd fueled her writing; her ability to make light of it made her writing exceptional. Her acceptance of 'life's essential unfairness', allowed her to reinvent herself and begin a new literary career, one unfairly neglected in public opinion.[18]

1: Selina Hastings, *Nancy Mitford: A Biography* (New York: Vintage Books, 2012), 22.

2: Evelyn Waugh to Nancy Mitford, August 24, 1951, in *The Letters of Nancy Mitford & Evelyn Waugh*, ed. Charlotte Mosley (London: Hodder and Stoughton, 1996), 233.

3: Lisa Hilton, *The Horror of Love: Nancy Mitford and Gaston Palewski in Paris and London* (New York: Pegasus Books, 2011), 188.

4: Ibid., 207.

5: Nancy Mitford, *Madame de Pompadour* (New York: New York Review of Books, 2001), 94.

6: Ibid., 87.

7: Nancy Mitford to Evelyn Waugh, June 6, 1946, in *The Letters of Nancy Mitford & Evelyn Waugh*, ed. Charlotte Mosley (London: Hodder and Stoughton, 1996), 42.

8: Ibid., 42.

9: Evelyn Waugh to Nancy Mitford, June 11, 1946, in *The Letters of Nancy Mitford & Evelyn Waugh,* ed. Charlotte Mosley (London: Hodder and Stoughton, 1996), 45.

10: Nancy Mitford to Heywood Hill, November 12, 1952, in *Love From Nancy: The Letters of Nancy Mitford,* ed. Charlotte Mosley (London: Hodder and Stoughton, 1993), 362.

11: Nancy Mitford to Evelyn Waugh, *The Letters of Nancy Mitford & Evelyn Waugh*, ed. Charlotte Mosley (London: Hodder and Stoughton, 1996) 296.

12: Evelyn Waugh to Nancy Mitford, *The Letters of Nancy Mitford & Evelyn Waugh*, ed. Charlotte Mosley (London: Hodder and Stoughton, 1996), 300.

13: Nancy Mitford, *Madame de Pompadour* (New York: New York Review of Books, 2001), 118.

14: Nancy Mitford to Evelyn Waugh, *The Letters of Nancy Mitford & Evelyn Waugh*, ed. Charlotte Mosley (London: Hodder and Stoughton, 1996), 371.

15: Evelyn Waugh to Nancy Mitford, May 19, 1959, *The Letters of Nancy Mitford & Evelyn Waugh*, ed. Charlotte Mosley (London: Hodder and Stoughton, 1996), 413.

16: Selina Hastings, *Nancy Mitford: A Biography* (New York: Vintage Books, 2012), 106.

17: Nancy Mitford to Gaston Palewski, September, 1954, *Love From Nancy,* ed. Charlotte Mosley (London: Hodder and Stoughton, 1993), 392.

18: Nancy Mitford, *The Pursuit of Love* (New York: Vintage Books, 2010),12.

Sara Fowler is a 2013 graduate of Dickinson College, Pennsylvania. She has worked in public relations and marketing and is currently developing a biography of Evelyn Waugh and Nancy Mitford focusing on their friendship. She can be contacted at slfowler6@gmail.com.

HANNAH GARRARD

A Close War

THE LIBERIAN CIVIL WAR LASTED FOURTEEN YEARS, FROM 1989 TO 2003. It is a conflict I came to know well when, in 2006, I taught in a school on a Liberian refugee camp in Ghana. But while I was there I never discussed with Liberians their own memories of the war. It was not my war to bring up.

I had seen images on the news of the surreal costumes – wigs, frocks and dressing gowns – that the rebels wore. The tribal loyalties that divided Liberia were events I'd only read about. In 2005 after two years of peace, Liberia elected the first female African head of state. I read Ellen Johnson Sirleaf's memoir, and understood how a peaceful human being could end up working for Charles Taylor; she believed the country's finances were safer in her hands. I followed Charles Taylor's trial through the BBC and Al Jazeera – the despot who dictated the conflict from the forest, and intimidated Liberians into voting him into office. On screen he looked a sad, tired man; it was hard to believe he was capable of such systematic violence.

Karrus started the school on the camp where I worked – a Liberian refugee who spent eleven years in exile. We stayed friends after I left Ghana and in June 2014 I went to Liberia to see Karrus again. I was surprised when, after years of us never talking about the conflict, he shared with me his personal experiences. He was neither precious nor protective of the details. Nothing brought me closer to the war than those conversations I had with Karrus.

One conversation with him I remember clearly. It was late and we were on the porch of the guesthouse overlooking an empty concrete courtyard; the monsoon season had started and the first fat beads of rain had moved everyone inside. Karrus had a bag of mangoes that he wanted peeled for freezing. When they are ripe you can score the skin with a thumbnail, an eyelid opening, and slide the cool yellow fruit out in one move. We did a whole carrier bag like this, watching streaks of rain flash in the beam of the hurricane lamp. He told me about Taylor's rebels moving through the country.

'When you got to the checkpoint they'd just pick you out,' Karrus said. He put the mango in his lap and held up two fingers, like a gun. '*PAPAPAPAPAP!* In Careysburg they were chasing people like animals.' We had driven through Careysburg, north of Monrovia, earlier that day. A brief town, almost deserted. 'They shot the guy.' Karrus paused. 'They shot him and he dropped like he was dead. But he didn't die.'

Karrus had been my friend for a long time. I assumed he was somehow immune from witnessing such scenes; he always looked ahead into a bright vision of the future, and seemed eternally cheerful. But I know almost every adult Liberian has a story like this. He went on: 'When he got up, they followed the blood and chased him into the forest – all the way to Kakata. It was terrible.'

We continued scoring the mangoes in silence and eventually I asked him if he was at home, in Gbarnga, when the war began in December 1989. We were due to leave for our trip to his hometown the next day and I was worried it might stir difficult memories. 'I was not in Gbarnga when the war started,' Karrus said. 'I was here in Monrovia and the war got to my area, I think, July 1st 1990.' The date was stamped on his mind.

Charles Taylor had been on the scene for a while by 1990, planning a coup that would remove Samuel Doe from power. Throughout the 1980s Doe had governed Liberia as a dictator, persecuting and oppressing anyone who was not from the same Krahn tribe as him and fixing elections. Taylor wanted revenge, but for different reasons entirely. From 1983-1985 Taylor had been in prison in the US for stealing money from Doe's government. He absconded to the States after being discovered, but Doe had issued his arrest warrant. After mysteriously 'escaping' from his maximum-security jail in Boston (he'd bribed guards), Taylor returned to West Africa. For the next five years he travelled through Sierra Leone, Nigeria, Ghana and The Gambia recruiting soldiers to help him take power from Doe, promising them riches and comradeship. Taylor – an American-Liberian – was well connected: Colonel Gaddafi had agreed to help train Taylor's new recruits for guerrilla warfare in Libya, and The Ivory Coast's president supplied him with arms. Houphouët-Boigny had his own grudge against Doe; he had murdered his son-in-law.

On Christmas Eve 1989, Taylor's National Patriotic Front of Liberia (NPFL) invaded the country from the north through Nimba County, a central region of Liberia covered in mountainous jungle. Karrus is from Bong County, right in the centre of Liberia – the NPFL would have arrived there soon after invading. 'There is this beautiful waterfall in Bong,' he told me. 'It's the only thing the rebels could not destroy.'

Taylor was quick to establish a new band of Liberian recruits making their way to Monrovia in search of Doe's blood. They dressed in bizarre costumes – wedding dresses, wigs – to frighten people, and to mark themselves out as rebels. Some even believed their outfits had talismanic powers, giving them immunity from danger.

1990 was a terrifying year: when the NPFL arrived at villages, men were forced to join up or murdered. Women and girls were raped. Houses burned and looted. Taylor recalls a different story: 'As the NPFL came in,' he told reporters, 'we didn't have to act. People came to us and said: "Give me a gun. How can I kill the man who killed my mother?"' He galvanised large groups of men by opening the prisons and arming inmates. He went to orphanages and organised the notorious Small Boy Units. Images of children in oversized T-shirts holding up Kalashnikovs almost as big as they were made headlines all over the world. Drugged, they were able to kill without conscience.

On the refugee camp I had known young men who had been boy soldiers. They lived in their own community and went to rehabilitation sessions. On the allotments at the far boundary they grew cucumbers and peppers for selling door to door. They travelled around the camp with their vegetables for sale, showing everyone they were useful and sorry. I remember a young man called Georgie who used to visit me at home in the afternoons after I'd finished teaching. We'd play a Ghanaian game called Oware together in the shade of the overhanging roof. In Oware you drop dried beans into cups and try to take your opponent's, leaving them with nothing. It's a strategy game, but there is luck involved.

Georgie had no family on the camp. It was just him. He wanted to be an actor, he told me, so he could tell his story to the world. The scar running from his cheek to the corner of his mouth gave a sinister context to his life.

By June 1990 Monrovia was being attacked from the east by NPFL rebels, and from the west by a second group of insurgents. By September, Doe would be dead. Karrus was somewhere on the outskirts of Monrovia by this time and had been moving on as the NPFL closed in. He eventually found safety in a small district of Monrovia called Bong Mines where a German corporation was still in operation – mining iron ore and exporting it to Europe. They stayed in the city despite the encroaching violence. International companies had huge investments in Liberia, which is rich in timber and iron; they had a lot to lose by leaving.

'You know that July is a terrible time in Liberia for rain,' Karrus said. 'There's nowhere for shelter and everything just gets wet.' The rain that night sounded like far away thunder on the tin roofs across the city. He stood up and stretched, then continued: 'Somewhere round here is a military barracks. We left from there and went to Careysburg. Again, trouble. So we went to Bong Mines. We were safe; we had the Germans there, we used their supermarket and we stayed in the house all day with the AC watching movies. You could go to the supermarket and come back – the rebels were around but they were not really doing anything.'

I wondered which movies Karrus watched – did he remember? I didn't ask. Ironic, I thought, how all the drama was happening on a screen. We assume war is all about action. But in reality, off screen, it is tedious. In between bursts of combat, life is halted, inert. We don't think of war zones as boring.

Monrovia was under attack and the city had no power or running water; people began to starve. Around half of Liberia's population was internally displaced and people were leaving the country any way they could – on buses, boats, or just running to the border. America sent a Navy rescue vessel, but saved only foreigners.

The Buduburam refugee camp, where I met Karrus, was set up by the UNHCR. It began life as a few rows of white tents, but grew bigger each day as people arrived in their hundreds. No one imagined the camp would still be there in eighteen years' time.

I asked Karrus what happened when the Germans left Bong Mines.

'As soon as they went the story changed,' he said. 'The rebels started killing people, dogs, and looting. I think they killed because,' he paused, choosing his words carefully, 'to show their power. To create fear in everyone else.'

Karrus stood to shake out the mango juice from the empty carrier bag –
we had a good pile now. We rested our feet on the low wall, leaning back in
our plastic chairs. The downpour had raised the drain level and a sweet
stench rose up. The humidity draws smells from the earth here. Karrus
explained how during the war the rebels became paranoid and started
killing people over trivialities – a look, a word, as if there were no rules.

'Sometimes you are *not* Mandingo or Mano.' He spoke as if the war
were happening right now. 'But they see you are very black and say you
are a criminal. They see you are wearing socks and decide you are military
personnel. If they see your hair is very clean they say "Hey! you are a
recruit – you're going to join the army to come and kill us." People are all
wicked in different directions.'

'Not everybody is wicked,' I said.

Karrus's phone rang, a frantic tune that cut across our conversation.
He went to take the call inside. I was left alone on the porch with the piled
up mangoes, watching the relentless June rain soak the city.

Hannah Garrard grew up in Suffolk and studied English Literature at UEA in
2005. She has taught English in West Africa, South Korea and the UK and is
now a youth and community worker in Norfolk. Her writing has been published in
The Guardian, *New Internationalist* and *Going Down Swinging*. She is currently
writing about Liberia.

MARTHA HENRIQUES

The Lark

THE CAPTIVE WAS MATURE WHEN IT ARRIVED, ITS JUVENILE FLUFF SHED for mottled brown and black plumage.[1] The lark had a whitish-yellow breast that complemented the flowers it ate from the children's palms, drawing almost hypnotic attention. Emily, the eldest, stayed up to sketch the bird while her younger brother Mackworth straggled more daisies through the bars.

Mackworth ran to and fro in the garden with glee at receiving his new pet. His favourite caterpillars and wasp nests thrived on this diversion as he collected spiders and picked at plants to try the lark on. Emily was unimpressed, and distracted herself with a new botanical discovery.[2] In the warm, wet climates of the south of the United States of America there were carnivorous plants that could snap up Mackworth's insects. Venus fly traps could clamp shut their jaws on dead flies or even strips of dried meat, slowly digesting their meal over a course of days.[3] Probably his fingers too, she considered, as he ran past again.

Mackworth's morbid excitement at the caged animal repulsed Emily, but the bird seemed placid enough. It moved slowly about the bottom of its cage, now littered with a selection of Mackworth's garden offerings. Emily made a point of avoiding the room where he sat to pester the lark into the night. She opened a compendium on caged birds. There were more than thirty-three types of lark native to the British Isles, she

---

1: Gates, B. (ed), *Journal of Emily Shore*, Virginia: University Press of Virginia (1991) p. 51

2: Gates, B. (ed), (1991) p. 51

3: Gates, B. (ed), (1991) p. 51

read.[4] She pushed a curled gold strand behind her ear. Mr Tebbut hadn't said which kind this was. None of the images immediately stood out to her. The bird had had a modest crest, she remembered, but from that alone she couldn't be sure which of several breeds it was. Mackworth's cackles filtered down to the hearth. The pleasure the boy gained from the animal's confinement was nauseating. She turned more pages. Perhaps she could go to identify the bird and minimise his persecutions at the same time.

She followed the boy's shrieks to the aviary and entered, calming Mackworth with a few questions. She sat down before the cage and looked through the entries. The bird preened, and Mackworth quietened down, watching. She stopped. 'Bill brownish-black, with the base of the lower mandible ochreous-yellow.'[5] She looked up over the pages at the bird. It really was beautiful. She entreated Mackworth to fetch her sketch pad and pencils. To her surprise he did. 'Above the eye is a yellowish-white streak. Cheeks pale yellowish-brown. Breast pale wood-brown, spotted with brownish-black; the middle white, with a reddish-brown tinge.' She stopped reading. It was a sky lark. The pad and pencils were in her hands and Mackworth settled behind her shoulder. She began to sketch. The bird hopped from the cage floor to its perch, displaying to Emily the plumage of each of its wings and its crest in turn, and returning to the water basin to hook its toes on the edge, bend down, and tilt its head over the water without drinking. She wondered what the natural territory range was for a lark. She glanced to the book in Mackworth's lap and saw he was looking at a page on linnets. She snapped shut her notebook and left him propped against the wall beneath the window. The house would be full of cages soon.

Thick fog early the next morning obscured Emily's hope for rambles in the garden.[6] The dawn chorus seemed correspondingly muffled anyway. She dawdled her way back to the bird room. Mackworth had already let both lark and goldfinch out of their cages. Offended by the audacious newcomer, the tiny finch had fluffed out his feathers with bravado and screamed his indignation.[7] The lark tried to avoid its outrage, flying over

4: Bolton, J. (1830) pp. 16

5: Excerpts from Prideaux, J. S., *Land Birds*, Edinburgh: W H Lizars (1825) p. 275

6: Gates, B. (ed), (1991) p. 51

7: Gates, B. (ed), (1991) p. 57

the children's heads to a corner of the high, dark ceiling. The unremitting defender of the aviary bickered with insistence until the lark retaliated. The larger bird attempted to beat off its small and ferocious enemy. It failed and quickly retreated further into its corner of the room, struggling to find a perch anywhere on the walls, settling for the frame of a portrait. Mackworth cackled, and Emily sided with the more timid bird, gaping and screeching at the goldfinch from its relative safety.[8]

The defending champion fluffed its feathers a little more and invaded the lark's empty cage, dipping its short beak in its water. Heady with success, the goldfinch plundered his enemy's hempseed and failed to appreciate the lark's own stealthy revenge in response, as it flew down to enter the other empty cage to peck at the unguarded seed.[9] Emily stayed quiet while Mackworth jeered at the birds, but the show was too good not to watch to the end. The birds seemed to forget about each other eventually after seeming to reach a stalemate, safe in one another's abodes.

Settling into the house over the next few days, the lark was welcomed into the breakfast room to forage for crumbs.[10] The children purposefully brushed them onto the floor by their chairs for it; none more than Mackworth, whom the lark nonetheless chose to avoid. Visitors to the lark's room in turn were greeted with a wide open beak, soon closed with resentment if there was no offering of a fly. The lark chirped and perched close to anyone there, except Mackworth, whose initial affection for the lark was quickly subsiding into crueller curiosity and provocation. Emily scolded him for teasing the bird with flies out of reach beyond the cage. Regardless, she would be followed down the corridor from the aviary by her brother's giggles and the increasingly familiar screech of warring birds.

Wet but less foggy mornings approached, and Emily continually scolded herself for lying in bed until five, missing most of the birdsong by the time she was out.[11] On these occasions she wandered once again to the bird room. The first time the lark landed on her hand its round, puffed body was impossibly, deceptively light. One could appreciate even up close the movements of its head were almost too quick to see, appearing to change from one instant to another between attitudes. Emily encouraged

8: Gates, B. (ed), (1991) p. 52, 57–58
9: Gates, B. (ed), (1991) p. 57–58
10: Gates, B. (ed), (1991) p. 57
11: Gates, B. (ed), (1991) p. 53

the bird from one hand to the wrist of the other, while she reached for the notebook. Her pencil scratched the paper propped on her bent knee. Minutes passed and the bird didn't leave her wrist, though she shifted it every now and then to let the delicate claws rest on a different patch of skin.

After three weeks in the house the lark was becoming less manageable. It would fly at its tormentor if he entered the room, berating him, pecking at his fingers, and pursuing the boy out of the room with screams.[12] Even Emily was subject to pecking fits if Mackworth was in the room. The moment he scampered from the aviary the lark would return to her, become dainty and polite, and eat quietly out of her hand. Mackworth monitored his pet's mutinous allegiance to his sister. He took increasing satisfaction in unleashing the goldfinch in her absence.

By the June of its confinement the lark had developed an unignorable series of eccentricities, becoming an increasingly exacting house guest. Certain frocks of Emily's were no longer acceptable. If she didn't wear its preferred dress, or if she arrived with dirty hands from gardening, or if she brought the wrong kind of fly, the bird would fly around the room to perch elsewhere and gape and screech at her, avoiding her fingers and outstretched hands.[13]

While Mackworth now boycotted the room entirely for his own safety, Emily decided to wait out the bird's wrath. Besides, she had read that 'the lark during the summer months is decidedly unsocial.'[14] She tried to explain to Mackworth, whose offence mingled openly with hurt and jealousy. 'For though we may meet with two or three pairs in the same field, we seldom find their nests near each other. They are not quarrelsome and pugnacious, like the red-breasts, but they seem to prefer a secluded spot to a crowded neighbourhood.' Perhaps with a little more peace the bird would be happier, she suggested. 'The young larks, after leaving the nest, seem equally unsocial, and do not, like most nestlings, keep together in a band; but prefer to wander about the field by themselves, though this must increase the trouble of their parents in bringing them food.' Not for our pampered visitor, she thought. 'Yet these seemingly unsocial birds, as soon as the breeding season is fully over, flock together in numbers almost incredible, and have then been

12: Gates, B. (ed), (1991) p. 59

13: Gates, B. (ed), (1991) p. 59

14: Extracts from Rennie, J. *The Domestic Habits of Birds*, London: Charles Knight (1833) pp. 657

caught for the table in most countries of Europe from the earliest times.'
She stopped reading. Perhaps the bird's mood was seasonal, and might
stand a chance of passing if the creature forgot Mackworth.

Able to take a hint, he ostentatiously turned his interest back to his old
amusements in the garden. While he lay sullenly on his front examining
a slow and unstimulating caterpillar outside, there was another's voice in
the garden, its enthusiasm rendering no need for a partner. Emily stage
whispered to herself as she investigated the undergrowth.[15] The bushes
by the border sheltered all kinds of weeds that the bird might yet like to
try. She had just finished reading *Hamlet* and she recited as she gathered,
picking rosemary for remembrance, pansies for thought.[16] The grass was
damp. Emily stooped and a cough rose up in her chest. The summer had
been wet and cool so far and the herbs had grown surprisingly well.[17] She
picked a brittle stalk and added it to her bundle.

She was done, ready to take the feast to the cage. She stopped her
whispering when she thought she heard someone calling to her. A cough
came over her again as she ran into the house and up the stairs and
she supported herself on the shiny surface of the thick, dark wooden
bannister.[18] She wiped curls from her eyes and checked the prize bundle
was still intact before entering the room. Mackworth wasn't there.
The bird was moving from one perch in its cage to another, repeating
a measured rocking motion at each of the furthest points of the cage.
Emily arranged her flowers and approached while the bird accelerated its
motion, keeping to precisely the same pattern and dipping its head with
each repetition. Emily hadn't noted this behaviour before and hesitated
at the bars, watching for a while. It showed no signs of stopping. She
decided to alleviate the poor bird of what must have been its anticipation
for the feast in her hands. She opened the cage door to offer a small sprig
of rosemary and interrupt its dance.

The force with which the bird clamped down its slightly serrated beak
drew down hard on the end of her finger, catching the soft part before the
bed of the nail.[19] The rosemary fell from her hands. There was no blood

---

15: Gates, B. (ed), (1991) p. 59

16: Gates, B. (ed), (1991) p. 22, 59, 223

17: Gates, B. (ed), (1991) p. 43

18: Gates, B. (ed), (1991) p. 28, 59

19: Gates, B. (ed), (1991) p. 57–58

but the skin was blue-white from the brief pressure, and soon flashed red and became swollen. Tiny flaps of skin were raised from the beak's ridges. The rest of the flowers scattered around Emily's feet.

Martha Henriques is a journalist and non-fiction writer. This extract is from her biography of the nineteenth-century natural historian Emily Shore, who died of tuberculosis aged 19. Despite barely reaching the end of childhood, Shore lived intensely through her botanical investigations, publications, and diaries.

LAURA LOVETT

Finding the Octopus

'THIS COOKIE… TASTE… TASTE LIKE LAPTOP,' THOMAS SAID, TILTING HIS head and smiling at me with gap teeth. Thomas Jefferson had quite a lofty name to live up to; after all, his namesake wrote the Declaration of Independence. My Thomas Jefferson didn't speak much and when he did he usually didn't make a whole lot of sense. He was small boned and darker than my other students. But it was his words that made him stand out; all jumbled up and framed by a toothy smile.

I'm dyslexic so I understood some of Thomas's plight, perpetually getting words and lines mixed up and out of order creating a new image. When I was in first grade the words on the page all blobbed together and made blocky shapes instead of meaning. I was chubby with a mushroom haircut so I couldn't risk any other social dilemmas. Instead, I made up my own stories during read out louds. Rather than Jill and Bill riding the red wagon I decided to entertain the class and cover up the fact I couldn't read. I inserted new phrases that I had heard about a Bill the night before on TV. 'Bill is not having sexual relatives with that wagon.' I wasn't sure exactly what it meant but I remember my sister saying never to repeat the phrase about 'sexual relatives'.

Eventually the letters came into focus for me and I decoded or memorized the shapes of words and fitted them to meaning. But I still experiment with words, trying to work out placement with a swing and a miss. A few years ago I was on a first date and told a man that I saw a 'defecated building on the way. It was really sad.' When the man spat out his drink I decided I might have used the wrong word. A few days later I realized I meant to say 'dilapidated'. I ended up loving words.

I met Thomas when I was teaching English in one of the poorest schools in North Carolina. He sat in the back row of my inclusion class. This class was made up of students with learning disabilities or behavioral issues, and mainstream learners. On the second day of school Thomas informed me that a blank piece of paper 'looks like… like my brother.'

At the time I was a twenty-three-year-old first year teacher. The school couldn't find another teacher to instruct this class so they put me in there to give it a go. A boy with a police-issued tracking ankle bracelet sat in the front row and next to him was a girl who was thirteen but behaved like a three year old. A lot of the time Thomas didn't get the attention he needed because I was busy trying to control my class. An average day went a bit like this:

Me: 'Your warm-up is to describe someone at home in four sentences using four senses: sight, smell, touch, hearing.'

'What about them taste?' Lashawn, a smart aleck would pipe up, 'Don't you taste someone at home? I see your knees is all red. You down on them knees licking your boy?'

They never taught me how to deal with this in training.

'Absolutely not Lashawn. That's a call home.'

But no matter how disorganized and disruptive the class was, Thomas always entered very astute. He came in and took out his pencil set, used notebook and erasers then folded his hands waiting for me to begin.

*

He had a special education case manager, Ms Hoyt. She was a first year teacher too and had about five weeks of training like me. A few months into school I approached her about Thomas.

She invited me into her office, which had been a supply closet until the beginning of the school year when the administration kicked the janitor out and put in the Special Education staff. It still smelled like Pine-Sol solution.

'What's up?' she asked.

'I had a few questions about Thomas Jefferson. I see on his learning plan he gets extra time for tests and I can repeat directions.'

'Yup,' she smiled, 'what is your question?'

'His speech is very fragmented… and it's… it's not accurate is it? I mean he told me that a piece of blank paper looked like his brother.'

'I have noticed,' she said hesitantly.

'Does he have a speech diagnosis?'

She pursed her lips together and brushed her wispy hair out of her face. 'No,' her voice grew tense, 'you know what the budget is like here. The school will never get a speech therapist.'

'What do you think it might be? Did you go over anything like this in training?'

'I can't really comment, Miss Lovett. Just give him extra time on the test and see if he needs things explained again.'

*

Why was biddy not going to do anything?

Wait – did I really think biddy? I did. My language was expanding with new vocabulary seeping in. My students introduced me to brilliant new words that seemed to fit certain situations better than any vocabulary I had.

Ratchet was one of my favorite words. Ratchet typically refers to something that is broken down. The kids called my classroom decor ratchet because the shades had taken quite a beating and my posters were torn down after many violent outbursts.

Because I loved to try out new words I practiced a few of them with the kids. One of my favorite students pulled me aside one day and said to me, 'Mizz Lovett, you so funny with them up-itdy words. I'll teach you how to talk black. Bys the end of this year you be twerking.'

I was honored that my student had thought so much as to organize a private tutorial for the two of us. But at the same time I was worried. Did the kids see me as speaking another language? Other teachers used slang, no matter their socioeconomic and racial background, but was it right?

I didn't want kids to feel there was such a thing as talking 'black' or 'white'. Language comes from our community, our parents and in many ways our socioeconomic background. The student who wanted to teach me how to 'talk black' was primarily surrounded by black and Latino peers and saw white people only in a teacher role so they assumed language had set racial profiles. The linguistic rhythms many of my students had been brought up with made a lot of sense and fitted together quite beautifully.

However, I also realized that if my students were going to a job interview later on in life, using the word 'ratchet' was going to get them an instant rejection.

I knew that Goldman Sachs and Bank of America didn't care about being linguistically sensitive during their interviews. I ended up teaching with 'proper' English and throwing in a piece of slang now and again, when appropriate. I don't know if it was right or wrong. I still don't.

What I did know is that for a lot of my students language was hard and English class was the most difficult class for them. Words fitted together in a different sequence than they heard at home. A lot of the words that the kids weren't exposed to were the complex vocabulary of academia.

Sometimes Thomas's struggle with language was brushed aside as a typical language deficiency that most of the kids had. But I knew it was more than that – something wasn't connecting. And the odds were already against him so I tried to give him some special attention.

*

I never questioned Thomas's intelligence. He loved nature books. Especially the ones made up of photographs with lengthy explanations beside them. His favorite animals were the most ferocious ones – bears – sharks – venomous snakes.

In March I taught my non-fiction unit using National Geographic Kids and picked out all of the most terrifying animals to teach.

In one of my classes I focused on lions.

'What do lions eat?' I asked.

'They eat them boo out,' Lashawn piped up.

'Really? Really guys? We're talking about lions and y'all have to make it sexual. Come on people at least pretend like you're ready for the seventh grade.' I paused, 'Look in the text. Paragraph three.'

I let the class go silent.

'Carnivores,' I heard a very tiny voice say.

'What is that?' I asked.

'Carnivores,' Thomas Jefferson repeated.

'Yes, yes that's right, Thomas. They are carnivores.'

He nodded, 'Eat meat.'

*

April in the American south is hot. My car air conditioner broke and by the time I got to school I was dripping in sweat.

Inside the school was not much better; legally they were supposed to have air conditioning but it was broken and when things broke at Wilson they didn't get fixed. I noticed a lot of the kids still wearing sweatshirts and long trousers. Thomas wore a black sweatshirt everyday and black jeans to match.

Thomas never said that he was hot but had melodramatic pretend faints.

When I lined the kids up for a bathroom trip, Thomas would get out of his seat then put his hand over his forehead and collapse back into his chair.

I called his mother to discuss his clothing. The call went as follows:
'Hello, is this Thomas's mother?'
'Yeah, who's this?'
'This is Miss Lovett, his English teacher. Thomas is having daily faints. I think he is just being dramatic. I think it's because of his clothes – we have—'
'Give em a flooze shot.'
'I can't give him a flu shot. I'm not a nurse. I think—'
'Give em Peptal Bismal.'
'I don't think that's going to help.'
'Sorry mam, I can't do anything about it. I gotta go.'

*

At the end of the year Ms Hoyt gave me some insight into Thomas's future. She invited me back into the closet office for an end of the year update on my students. The smell of the Pine-Sol had faded and the room was now cluttered with colorful inspirational posters. She sat in front of a neon pink owl poster that said 'I'm a Hoot.'
'I talked to Thomas's mother. She seems to have some speech issues too,' I said.
'I've talked to her too. It could just be education. You know how it is here.'
'It's really sad. It might be a language processing disorder.'
She shrugged, 'Could be, but in this school it doesn't matter what it's labeled.'

'But I worry about what will happen to Thomas when he gets out of school.'

'Don't worry about Thomas. He'll go through the Special Ed department and they do a work placement.' She smiled. 'When he gets out he'll be set up with a job as a janitor or cashier. You know Thomas, he never makes a fuss. He'll take home a pay check and be happy as a clam. If you think about it he'll be doing better than most of our students.'

Better than most of our students; better than jail was what she meant. That was why no one in the school thought it was important to teach the language for a corporate interview, because it was understood that none of them would need to use big words to impress. It wasn't Hoyt's fault. She was a first year teacher like me and didn't have any resources either.

*

On one of the last days of school I gave the students a writing assessment to gauge their personal growth. The question was: What do you want to do with your life? What steps will you take to achieve this goal?

This time Thomas wasn't writing but looking out the window.

'What are you thinking about, Thomas?' I asked him.

'I want to go outside.'

'Not right now. What about the question? What do you want to do when you grow up? Do you want to work with animals?'

'Go... go on a journey,' he said.

'Do you want to be an explorer? Go on lots of journeys?'

He shook his head. 'One big journey,' he paused then added, 'and see an octopus too.'

Laura Lovett is a memoirist and journalist. At twenty-four she 'retired' from teaching determined to write about her experiences in a low income school in her memoir *When Everything Has Gone South*. She has a completed memoir entitled *Sass in the Spires* about her experiences dating Oxford men and crashing their boats.

KAYLA SCHMIDT

Dragonfly Weekend

THERE IS ONLY ONE PLACE IN NORTH DAKOTA WHERE THE ALTITUDE requires a forced yawn to pop your ears in order to stabilize the pressure that builds during ascent. The Turtle Mountains remain the one area for miles that can be described as 'wooded'. Everything else is wheat and highway.

Driving there takes about an hour and a half from my hometown. Our family cabin resides next to Lake Metigoshe, nestled in the forest of the Turtle Mountain region. Metigoshe is the biggest of the area's lakes, and a good portion of it is technically located in Canada.

'Alcohol down!' shouts my dad over the grumbling motor of our ancient pontoon. I think 'pontoon' is technically the term for the metal tubes that support the platform of the boat, but we're not much bothered by technicalities. Ours has two long benches parallel to these supports, the driver's seat, a small table and a bench that runs along the back. Too many folks at the front means any waves from passing speedboats or even particularly windy days will catch on the weighed down bow. Booze cruisin' on the lake is allowed (why drinking and driving is so heavily monitored on land yet law enforcement looks the other way when it occurs on water where there are A) no lanes, B) no speed limits, C) a risk of sinking, D) a risk of drowning, makes no sense to me). Except in the Canadian area of the lake. The Canadian 'Game and Fish Department' take this rule seriously. As soon as we enter international waters – there is no official marker, my dad estimates the distinction by means of a particular oak across the bay and the adornment of maple leaf flags on every surface of every cabin – we make sure to set any adult beverages below eye level, tucking them behind our feet or under life jackets.

'All clear!' comes the captain's call as we exit Canadian territory. Sunburnt arms reach to retrieve beers and ciders. Condensation on the sides of bottles attract stray sunflower seed hulls.

'That one. I've always loved that one. Look at the dormer windows and the green shingles. It's just so lakey,' my mom says, pointing at a lakefront property. She's always on the lookout for the perfect cabin.

'It's good, but I don't like the honey-stain. I want something a little more red,' replies my dad. He's removed his shirt and cracker crumbs are sticking to his graying chest hair. He spends much of his summer working outdoors and has a fairly even tan except for the deep smoking-wrinkles that run down his cheeks. If he puffs his face out so the grooves flatten, they are stark white.

My parents don't agree on much except watching reruns of *Everybody Loves Raymond* and cozy-cottage style architecture. The recent oil boom and subsequent instant riches of North Dakota have meant a lot of new multi-level cabins with stone slab patios and numerous watercrafts parked on the beach outside.

'Who'd want to clean *that* every weekend? I don't even like doing the dishes up here. Can you imagine trying to clean all those windows?' my mom admonishes in disgust. She'd attempted to pull her hair in a ponytail to keep it off her shoulders, but wisps are beginning to come loose. Her swimsuit straps are stretched across her freckled shoulders. She's generally barefoot in the summer, her toenails colored a muted strawberry.

'Plus everybody keeps chopping down the trees and pouring concrete. You need a good lawn up here. There's never anybody home either. They spend all that money, raise our property taxes, and never show up. That's not what lakin's all about,' my dad steers into a new bay.

From far away, passing boatists probably imagine our cabin is the cozy ideal. It has beautiful chestnut wood siding. The gutters are painted dark green to match the lattice work below the deck. The lawn is mowed, albeit scattered with chairs and gossip magazines.

My parents hope that the cabin will meet a natural disaster so they can rebuild. The place has existed for a mighty long time given its questionable origins. We don't know who built it or how it's managed to stay upright. The foundations include several crumbling cinderblocks and mostly cobwebs. During rainy evenings we play 'find the leak'. Each year we add at least two more buckets to the game.

'Girls, come look at how much the floor's tilted now,' my dad inevitably mentions once a weekend. The contracting and expanding of wood in damp and hot months causes the bathroom floor to shift, a change his eagle eyes never fail to register. 'I'll bet that toilet's tilted another thirty degrees since last summer.'

My dad rarely sits during the weekends. He says the cabin is his one true escape, the only place he can relax, but at every turn he's holding a weed-wacker or a paintbrush. He never asks if we want to help chop wood or stain the deck. I don't think it's exclusion on account that he only has three daughters, rather simply his own way of clearing his head. Sharing his love of Metigoshe is his most obvious way of expressing tenderness. He's the first to usher us out to watch a baby fawn. He's the one who keeps the hummingbird feeders full of sugar water. Observation of change appeals to him in a strong way.

*

Amongst the many Schmidt home videos – a gratuitous stack of VHS tapes collecting dust in the basement – plenty take place at Der Schmidt Haus (a nod to our German heritage, this moniker is painted on plenty of surfaces of the cabin). Toddler Kristin, my twin sister, calls out to me across the sand. Metigoshe's water levels are dependent on run-off from Canada. Most of our childhood occurred during a drought that left lake levels low and provided a wide beach.

'Here's one!'

'Let me see, Krissy,' inspects Grandma. 'Yep. Stomp on it.'

'Stomp. Stomp. Stomp.' Kristin uses her foot while I use a plastic shovel to eradicate whatever creature has invaded our sacred property.

Mom would always try to encourage us to respect nature. But nature itself isn't kind. Mosquitos are a problem in the Turtle Mountains. They feast on campers, pets, and wildlife. The damp environment provides plenty of puddles for egg-laying. Citronella candles don't deter mosquitos. Nor does the gallon of bug repellant I coat myself in every weekend. Our only savior is the dragonflies.

It took me plenty of years to appreciate them. They'd storm our bay almost exclusively. Dragonfly weekend is the first true mark of summer. Thousands of nymphs crawl out of Lake Metigoshe where they've waited, submerged in the water, until the weather conditions are right.

The creatures my sister took great pleasure in stomping in that family video were dragonfly nymphs. At this point they are scaly, ugly, and look as if they are coated in dirty tissue paper. A dragonfly's wings cannot open until it has shed this shell. The insects align themselves in great columns amongst the bark of trees. Hordes of them cling to the rusted mesh of screen doors on the cabins that surround the lake. Any surface with sufficient texture lures the sodden creatures.

I remember inspecting them as they attached their spindly legs to the chicken wire my parents had lined the elevated deck with when we were children. While accidents are expected at the cabin, my mom was incredibly wary of us crawling below the railing to our doom.

*

I helped my dad inspect the cabin roof last summer. By 'help' I mean he left the ladder unattended and I climbed up to see the view. The roof slopes in odd spots, the shingles have shifted after being battered by wind and blizzards and determined squirrels who run across the expanse every morning, collecting acorns from a gnarled oak on the east side of the cabin for their stash somewhere on the west.

'It seems a lot smaller from up here,' I announce, scraping olive-colored moss off a torn shingle with the front of my sandal.

'It's getting to be more work than it's worth. We're just playing keep-up at this point. Stay at least two feet away from the edge. You're making me nervous.'

How my parents could ever imagine replacing this testament to family history, I cannot fathom. The green shag carpet, the wood paneling, the Big Mouth Billy Bass hanging behind the bright orange fireplace – it's Americana kitsch like Hollywood or a very specific kind of museum could never recreate.

*

Some dragonflies don't make it beyond the first stages. If they can't find a safe place to climb, they run the risk of being trod on. Once securely attached, a dragonfly will emerge from its casing. They fall backwards out of their shell, arms crossed – like a mummy emerging from a sarcophagus or an astronaut whose sleeping bag has come undone in space. Free to maneuver, their crumpled wings lengthen and shudder as they prepare for flight.

Occasionally, a novice dragonfly will dive too close to the lake's surface. Never mind survival of the fittest, I happily spend the weekend rescuing the poor darlings. Once when I was five years old, the neighbors' dog knocked me into the lake. I knew how to swim, but I wasn't expecting the blow and I panicked until someone pulled me up by the loops of my jeans. A drowning dragonfly will grasp onto the end of an extended twig. I'll wade into the lake up to my knees or lie on my belly across the dock to reach those in peril. I safely deposit the bug in a sunny spot, specifically designated to rehabilitate sodden insects. They crawl onto the grass with gratitude and let their wings dry.

There's something incredibly fragile about the creatures, something about how they are entirely reliant on their environment despite all the indirect hostility nature has in store. The air is cluttered with tentative first-time fliers. When the sun is shining, the light seeps through their translucent wings and casts delicate silhouettes on the ground. These iridescent creatures bear little resemblance to their previous state. The shells that have been shed remain affixed to every vertical surface for the remainder of the summer. As children, they terrified my sisters and me. We didn't understand that they were empty. They crunched if you brushed up against them. We couldn't connect the relation between the dragonflies that landed on our fingertips if we stood still for long enough and the minuscule monsters attached to the side of the gazebo that stared at us through crusty, unblinking eyes.

One spring, a massive wind storm swept through the mountains. The biggest damage occurred to the great aspen tree in the middle of our yard. One of the tallest in the bay, the gusts had tipped it over. This should have been the cabin's undoing had the deck railing not stopped it from falling further. Cleaning the damage, dragonfly shells fell like snow. The bark of the aspen had been their favorite location to sun. Each gloved hand removing debris crushed generations' worth of shells. Accumulation. That's what makes Metigoshe special. Each year another stray spoon finds its way into our cutlery drawer, another layer of paint maintains the cabin's cracking façade, more nymph shells line the lake's landscape.

We always leave our cabin on Sundays when the sun is low and the horizon seems like a myth. Confronted with the miles of flat always makes me squeamish and reluctant to head home. Right before you drive out of the mountains, the steep hill winding down emerges over a treeless ridge. The whole of North Dakota stretches in front of you in segregated patches of sepia. This filter makes the mountains seem so much more enchanting – with their bright blues and greens, slightly hidden, slightly dangerous and safe at the same time. Lake Metigoshe is full to the brim with nostalgia and stinky fish and plush seaweed and somewhere deep below, dragonflies ready to emerge.

Kayla Schmidt can't wait to plan her next adventure. Raised in the plains region of Midwest America (where not much happens), she finds excitement in all aspects of life. Whether it's contributing to the feminist movement, travelling the world, or questioning the mundane habits of everyday life, read about her experiences at foxyproxiewrites.tumblr.com.

ANN KENNEDY SMITH

Caroline's War

S HE CHARMED EVERY MAN SHE EVER MET. ON THE FIFTH OF JANUARY 1861 Caroline Slemmer sat down in her home, an army barracks in Florida, to write a letter to her married older sister Ellen. It was a breathless account of all the Christmas and New Year parties she had been to and the countless times she had been asked to dance, how she had conquered the heart of every officer there and triumphed over women who were prettier and better dressed than she was. Caroline was a vivacious, witty twenty year old with auburn hair who rather liked the idea that she resembled Thackeray's scheming Becky Sharp, although, as she said, Becky Sharp would do anything for money, she, nothing. She enjoyed the feeling of power that being the centre of male attention gave her, and boasted to her sister that one infatuated officer had called her a charming little sinner.

What Caroline's husband made of all this can only be imagined. He was a thirty-year-old army officer called Lieutenant Adam J Slemmer. A photograph of him from the time shows a slim, bearded man in uniform, arms folded self-consciously, his eyes wary behind rimless spectacles. Caroline was only sixteen when she married him, perhaps because army life seemed to promise the excitement and adventure she craved. Their son Bertie was born a year later and she adored him, but her marriage did not bring her much else in the way of happiness. In her long letters to her sister she hardly refers to her husband; it seems that there was nothing much to say about him.

The reality of being an army wife meant moving from barracks to barracks, living far away from her mother and sisters and with no time to build friendships. To pass the time she read, rode her horse and took German lessons, but the skill she worked hardest on was flirting. In the spring of 1860 she and Adam were sent to the military base of Fort Barrancas in the town of Pensacola in western Florida. The barracks overlooked the sparkling blue Gulf of Mexico which had white sandy beaches and year-round balmy temperatures. The nearby naval yard also meant that Caroline could practise deploying her charms on an even greater number of impressionable men. She discovered that naval officers were particularly grateful for attractive female company after months at sea, and every day several of them called to walk with her.

In her gossip-filled letters to her sister during this time, Caroline gives no indication that she was aware that the country was on the verge of civil war. Trouble had been brewing between North and South since Abraham Lincoln was elected President of the United States in November 1860 on a promise to abolish slavery. The Southern states wanted to break away from the Union and form their own separate Confederacy, and as President-elect Lincoln was working hard to find a peaceful means of keeping the United States together. All of his efforts were failing, and in December the state of South Carolina declared secession.

In Florida, the next state to secede from the Union, the situation had reached crisis point by the start of 1861. Armed Southern troops prepared to take control of all official United States property, including post offices, courts and the strategically important naval base and federal forts in Pensacola harbour. Fort Barrancas had been built to protect the United States from attacks from the sea. Now it faced an unprecedented threat from the land as the Confederates prepared to seize control, just at the time the commander and second-in-command of Fort Barrancas had gone on leave, leaving Caroline's husband in sole charge of this large military outpost. With a company of only fifty men, Adam Slemmer knew that he stood no chance of defending the fort successfully against thousands of Confederate soldiers.

On the fifth of January, he convened an emergency meeting of all the local military and naval officers in their house. Caroline stopped writing her letter and went to hear the men trying to decide on the best course of action. Should they surrender the forts and naval yard, and sail North? Or stay and fight a hopeless battle? The arguments for and against went on for hours. Eventually Caroline, who had been sitting quietly listening to the discussion, could stand it no more. 'Well, if you men will not defend your country's flag, I will!' she said, jumping to her feet.

Caroline's patriotic enthusiasm settled the matter for the men. Adam decided to move the entire company to a smaller fortification which they would defend until reinforcements were sent from the North. This was Fort Pickens, a disused fort on a windswept strip of land just off the Florida coast called Santa Rosa Island. Before leaving Fort Barrancas, they spiked the guns and destroyed over twenty thousand pounds of gunpowder. Then, leaving wives and family behind, Adam led a party of fifty soldiers and thirty sailors to Santa Rosa Island in a convoy of small boats loaded down with ammunition, provisions and an old mule and cart. They would spend the next four bleak months there. On the tenth of January Florida seceded from the Union, and on the twelfth the Confederates took charge of Fort Barrancas and the naval base.

In the midst of all this upheaval, Caroline somehow found a few moments to finish her letter to her sister. It was written in a very different tone to how she started it four days before. She describes how the little town of Pensacola feels warlike, its residents now openly hostile towards them, and she criticises the United States government for not sending orders or reinforcements. She says that she would be prepared to join her husband in Fort Pickens, no matter how bleak a place it is, and help him to defend it against Confederate attackers. The transformation is remarkable. In a matter of days Caroline has changed from a flirtatious young woman with her head full of parties to become a patriotic wife, prepared to stand at her husband's side and fight for the Union. In the end she did not have to. A safe escort was found, and she and the other wives packed up their luggage and set sail for New York with their children and servants.

The most exciting part of Caroline's war was just about to begin. When she arrived in New York she found that stories about her bravery had got there before her. One newpaper article described Caroline's beauty and brilliance in glowing terms, and said that she was worthy to be the wife of an American soldier. Another headline ran: *'Mrs Slemmer Arrested As A Spy'*. It was rumoured that she had tried to infiltrate Fort Barrancas to take notes and report back to her husband. Caroline's version of events was more believable, and only slightly less thrilling. She told a *Harper's Weekly* reporter that before leaving Penscola she had tried to go back into the barracks to fetch some of her husband's clothes, and when she was not allowed to enter she had threatened to return and man one of the guns herself. A Washington journal reported that Caroline's bravery had caused a sensation among the patriotic ladies there, who were preparing a suitable testimonial for her. Later that month she posed, looking beautiful and imperious, for a photographic portrait, and engravings of it were advertised for sale in newsagents. Caroline had become the Civil War's first patriotic pin-up.

While she was basking in all of this attention, Adam and his company were having a miserable time at Fort Pickens. The old fort was in a delapidated condition and the island was infested with rattlesnakes and vipers. Adam's company spent almost four months defending the fort against an invasion which never happened. When the long awaited federal reinforcements arrived in April many of the men were found to be suffering from scurvy. Their prolonged defence of this lonely outpost was worthwhile, however: Fort Pickens was one of the few Southern forts to remain in Union hands throughout the Civil War, and it was an important base for the North in the Gulf of Mexico during the blockade of the Southern states.

The first shots of the Civil War were actually fired at another besieged island six hundred miles away, Fort Sumter in Charleston Harbour, which was attacked by Confederate troops on the twelfth of April and forced to surrender two days later. The Fort Pickens siege was largely forgotten about after that, and Caroline's brief period of fame faded. She was all the more disappointed to discover after her husband returned that he was still a mere lieutenant, especially since she had read in the newspaper that less experienced men were being given commissions in the new military regiments. So once again she decided to take matters into her own hands. On the tenth of May she wrote to the President directly, suggesting that Adam should be recognised for his bravery at Fort Pickens. She was given an appointment to go to Washington DC to see Lincoln. Caroline's great-niece, Gwen Raverat, in her memoir *Period Piece*, tells the story that when her beautiful 'Aunt Cara', accompanied by her two brothers-in-law, went along to the arranged interview with the President they found him sitting at his writing table, working. The conversation was difficult at first; Lincoln was understandably preoccupied and perhaps Caroline let the men do the talking. So she did something very simple and very effective. She moved closer, put her hand lightly on the President's shoulder, and gently explained to him why she thought her husband should be promoted. Lincoln smiled, placed his hand on hers for a moment, and listened.

In the Abraham Lincoln papers at the Library of Congress there is a list in Lincoln's handwriting of the names of the officers he wished to promote that month. After the name Lieutenant Slemmer, Lincoln has scribbled a note: *'his pretty wife says a Major or First Captain.'* Adam Slemmer was made a Major soon afterwards, and Caroline had succeeded in charming the most important man in the land.

Sources

My thanks to Karen Kukil for permission to quote from the Lady Caroline Lane Reynolds Slemmer Jebb Papers, Sophia Smith Collection, Smith College, Northampton, Mass. I have also consulted Mary Reed Bobbitt's *With Dearest Love to All: The Life and Letters of Lady Jebb* (London: Faber, 1960) and Gwen Raverat's *Period Piece: The Cambridge Childhood of Darwin's Granddaughter* (London: Faber 1960). The Abraham Lincoln Papers at the Library of Congress for July 1861 can be found at the following web source: memory.loc.gov/cgi-bin/query/P?mal:2:./temp/~ammem_GlfT::(accessed 10 April 2015)

Ann Kennedy Smith lives in Cambridge where she teaches and writes on Victorian literature and art. She is currently working on *Cambridge Wives*, a biography of the group of women, including Ida Darwin, Mary Paley Marshall and Caroline Jebb, who came to Cambridge in the 1880s after university fellows were allowed to marry, and took the place by storm.

DEBORAH SPRING

Remembrances

S KERRY THE MASON WAS BALANCING HIGH ON THE ROOF OF WEST
Bilney Hall, replacing tiles, slowly making the house weathertight
after the winter storm that had shattered windows, lifted roofs and
flattened barns across England. The great wind of November last, 1703,
had been the worst Elizabeth Freke could recall since Oliver Cromwell
died, the worst for generations people said. A hurricane blast that
smashed ships to splinters, drowned thirty sailors in the harbour at
King's Lynn, and unthatched all the cottages on the Bilney estate. One of
her farmhouses was quite blown down. The tenants had stopped the gaps
and made good with odds and ends of timber and thatch straight after
the storm: that had cost her five hundred pounds and now it was spring
and there were more repairs to pay for.

Mistress of West Bilney Hall, Elizabeth managed the tenants and
tradesmen and trusted none of them. When she went in to fetch the
money from her closet to pay the mason, she knew her price. Six pounds
and no more. She would not be cheated, she was a match for them all.

Upstairs in the long, flint-faced house lay her husband Percy,
checkmated by gout and a rasping cough, in a high bed hung around with
green damask. Light was spinning across the room, dancing rainbows
over the gilt looking glass and catching the dark gleam of the tortoiseshell
cabinet opposite the bed. Percy Freke was propped on his wife's
best feather pillows, under the fine holland sheets she had reluctantly
unpacked from the locked chest in her closet, with a plaid quilt folded
at his feet. He had arrived to claim more money from her for his Irish
enterprises, but was now too ill to travel back to Cork.

Her husband was a rare presence at West Bilney. He had no time for the estate, or its meagre income from poor tenants.

'I'll sell it, I'll take the money to Ireland. This place won't keep me in bread and cheese,' he had shouted. That time, she saw and heard nothing more of him for two years. Seven times he had left her in empty houses with bare walls, her beds, sheets and money all taken. Now he could not walk a step, still less ride to Bristol and jump on a ship. Her unkind husband, who never in his life took any care for her or what she did.

She kept a journal, the account of her years of abandonment. On the first page she had written its title: 'The misfortunes that have attended me in my unhappy life since I were married.'[1] Elizabeth found no consolation in piety, and she never resigned herself to suffering. Indeed she re-examined her grievances, and retold her story with the addition of hindsight in a second version of the journal. Her November wedding day, the 'most grievous rainy, wet day' of the first telling, became in the later one 'a most dreadful rainy day (a presager of all my sorrows and misfortunes to me).'

*

Her son had not asked her consent or her blessing to his own marriage. She had never met her daughter-in-law Eliza, the woman who shared her name, or seen the two small grandsons in Ireland. 'For which I have and do forgive him, and wish him better fortune than I,' she wrote, remembering how she too had married without her father's consent. She had run away with Percy Freke all those years ago to marry for love, but he was not a loving man. She had soon learned that. Her orderly and thrifty father had been right, but it was too late.

It was March when the letter arrived from Eliza. She may have read it in the parlour, sitting by the polished oval table under the window. Along the wall was a fine cane settle. It had been a necessity when her sister gave it to her, the only piece of furniture she had after Percy disappeared with their money and possessions. The panelled room was comfortable

---

1: The source of this piece is Elizabeth Freke's journal, including household accounts and inventories, published as *The Remembrances of Elizabeth Freke 1671–1714*, edited by Raymond A Anselment. Cambridge, 2001. She lived at West Bilney, a Norfolk village about eight miles from King's Lynn.

now, hung round with four lengths of tapestry woven with green forest scenes. She had other tapestries folded away in chests, fine hangings, counterpanes and linens, and on the settle were silk embroidered cushions she had worked herself. Every closet, box and shelf in the house held its proper stock of the things she had slowly gathered together. A long portrait of her father hung above the fireplace, a flattened, varnished likeness of the man who had loved and protected her, given her the land at Bilney, and money that Percy had used up as soon as they were married.

Her daughter-in-law's brief letter told her that Ralph was suffering from dropsy. As no physician in Ireland could help him they were going to Bath for a cure, then would bring their children to visit Elizabeth and Percy. Although she knew it was not affection but illness that had woken them to think of visiting her, her hopes rose: would returning to his native country restore Ralph to her?

Ralph. His terrible birth, the child dismissed as dead, but saved by a midwife who caught a flicker of life in his face. She'd come out from Swaffham, and was kind and gentle, not like the man-midwife with his hard instruments and impatient ways who had wanted to drag out the baby. The baby's broken hip, the sickly childhood – he had been the focus of all her care and anxiety, her only living child. The year in Ireland at Rathbarry when he was an infant, the house bare and cold, her husband forever away, her mother-in-law cruel when she miscarried, no dear father or sisters to comfort her. She returned to England to bring Ralph up. But he left her to join his father in Ireland as soon as he was old enough to travel alone. Elizabeth was bereft.

It was autumn when Ralph and his family at last arrived at West Bilney. The man who greeted her was so big, so fat, so loaded with dropsical humour, she hardly recognised him as her son. Was Ralph as shocked when he saw his mother? She was disfigured by a recent fall from top to bottom of the stairs that had knocked out eight teeth, leaving only three in her upper jaw.

Her daughter-in-law Eliza was attended by her own servant, spent the mornings in her chamber with the door never quite shut, and was barely civil. She had never once troubled to greet her parents-in-law with a 'good morrow' or 'good night'. Finding her daughter-in-law so curt and aloof, Elizabeth turned to her grandsons. Her fondness for three-year-old John grew as the weeks passed; he quickly took first place with her. He was the picture of her boy Ralph, whom she still thought the loveliest child she ever saw, and seemed more real to her than his father, the bloated man who had stepped from the carriage a month before. Her mind filled with thoughts of her grandchildren and their future. When Ralph and Eliza went to visit their London friends would they leave the boys with her? She had asked them, more than once, but Eliza said nothing. Did she not know London was a bad place for children? Elizabeth wanted to keep John at Bilney.

While the maid tidied and dusted the room one morning, Elizabeth sat with Percy in the bedchamber. She mentioned a gift of fifty pounds they were planning to give Ralph. Before any answer came from him, the door was thrown open. There stood her daughter-in-law, flaring with temper.

'You should be ashamed to speak of such a trifling gift, and before a servant,' she shouted at Percy, then turned to Elizabeth, 'I've a good mind to kick your maid downstairs. You must turn her out of doors now, or I'll be gone myself...'

She must have been listening at the chamber door, thought Elizabeth.

*

The day of the departure, Elizabeth felt desperate. She pleaded with Eliza to leave the boys in her care. The city was full of disease, the children were not safe there. They could be left in the country until their parents were ready for the return to Ireland. But Eliza was impatient to be gone, and the coach took them all away to London.

How did the news reach her? She does not say. Ralph or Eliza must have summoned the courage to write, or perhaps they sent a messenger to explain. They told her how John and his brother were playing with a small boy called Tom in the London house where the family were lodging. Ralph's manservant was loading and priming a pair of pocket pistols. Suddenly Tom reached past him, snatching up a pistol: the gun exploded into life as he lifted it, the room filling with smoke, shouting and confusion. John had been standing near Tom, and took the full force of the explosion in his face. The bullet went through his eye, but he was still alive. His desperate parents sent for every surgeon and apothecary in London who might help, but it was no use. After three days he died, a month short of his fourth birthday.

Elizabeth collapsed when she heard of John's death, consumed with grief and anger: the dear child would not have died if he had been left with her. Her heart was broken, she had lost any comfort in this life. When John's body was brought to Bilney she moved without feeling through the day as she gave orders for the funeral. The church was full. The neighbours she had fought over debts and boundaries, the cheating tradesmen, all of them came. Afterwards she went into her bed, pulled the curtains round her, and lay there for many days, half sleeping, eating nothing, hearing the tolling of the passing bell which she had ordered to be rung for the dead child.

Ralph and Eliza stayed away. They took ship for Ireland without seeing Elizabeth and Percy again. Percy could not sleep, stand, or walk, and could barely breathe. Before long he too was dead, laid in the vault beside his grandson.

*

Dressed in a black gown and mantua, her hair under a plain cap, Elizabeth was finishing her inventory. She noted descriptions and quantities in neat columns: four pewter dishes, all good; one deep pewter dish, new; six dishes and six new trenchers; one round brass dish for a pie or pudding: recording everything in preparation for a long visit to her sister. She would take the road across the flat, empty marsh, where the summer shimmer of the reeds was over, dulled into grey by the low winter light. Her possessions were layered in chests and locked in closets: knotted turkey carpets, candlesticks, brass kettles, warming pans and chamber pots. Bottles of syrups, cordials and vinegar. Bowls and jars, bedlinen, aprons, mantuas, and waistcoats. Folded and nested, stacked and shelved, lying quiet in the dark, like memories waiting for their time to waken. Every room clean and undisturbed. In the dining room stood Elizabeth's own coffin, lined with lead, and the key to the vault. Hers would be the final funeral.

Deborah Spring was an academic publisher. Now she combines writing with consultancy. Her publications include a book and articles about early English gardens and garden-makers. As well as her work on Elizabeth Freke - possibly the original misery memoirist - current writing projects include the life of a sixteenth-century Hertfordshire woman; the biography of a house over five centuries; and a memoir.